JOB SAVVY

HOW TO BE A SUCCESS AT WORK

Instructor's Guide
Second Edition

LaVerne Ludden, Ed.D.
Marsha Ludden, M.A.

Job Savvy Instructor's Guide

© 1998 by JIST Works, Inc.

Published by JIST Works, Inc.
8902 Otis Avenue
Indianapolis, IN 46216
1-800-648-5478 E-mail: jistworks@aol.com
World Wide Web Address: http://www.jist.com

Other Books by LaVerne Ludden and Marsha Ludden

- *Job Savvy: How to Be a Success at Work*
- *Luddens' Adult Guide to Colleges and Universities*
- *Back to School: A College Guide for Adults*
- *Franchise Opportunities Handbook:*
    A Complete Guide for People Who Want to Start Their Own Franchise
- *Mind Your Own Business! Getting Started as an Entrepreneur*
- *Effective Communication Skills*
- *You Can Bank On It*

Other Products in This Series

- *Job Savvy: How to Be a Success at Work*
- *The How to Be a Success at Work Video Series:*
    You've Got the Job ... Now What?
    Working 9 to 5
    Career Tips for Your Future

See the back of this book for additional JIST titles and ordering information.
Quantity discounts are available.

Printed in the United States of America

3 4 5 6 7 8 9   02 01 00 99

We have been careful to provide accurate information throughout this book, but it is possible that errors and omissions have been introduced. Please consider this in making any career plans or other important decisions. Trust your own judgment above all else and in all things.

ISBN 1-56370-435-8

About This Book

Job Savvy is about keeping a job and getting ahead. It is based on research into what employers actually look for in the people they hire and designed to develop critical job survival skills, increase productivity, and improve job satisfaction and success. Using a workbook approach, the many activities reinforce key points and help develop new job survival skills and plans. The narrative is easy to read and informative with good graphic design, many examples, checklists, case studies, and section summaries.

In this second edition, *Job Savvy* has changed considerably while keeping the basic features that thousands of readers liked. The workbook changes are summarized in the "About This Book" section of *Job Savvy*. However, this *Instructor's Guide* contains even more changes and we think these changes will be appreciated by trainers, teachers, and other instructors.

The major changes to the *Instructor's Guide* include the following:

■ A guide for using the related three-part video series—*How to Be a Success at Work*

■ A test bank of 30 questions for every chapter in the workbook

■ A section describing how to use *Job Savvy* in a one-on-one training approach. This new content provides more instructional aids and makes it easy to use *Job Savvy* in either the classroom or workplace

■ 60 overhead transparency masters for you to copy.

Why People Need to Improve Their Basic Job Skills

The years ahead are projected to be a time of labor market opportunity and challenge for most workers:

■ Many new and existing jobs require higher levels of technical skills.

■ The amount of education and training required for jobs continues to increase.

- Employers expect employees to be more productive and get better results in more complex jobs.

- Employees are expected to take more responsibility for their careers.

All of these changes mean today's workers need to be better prepared than most workers have been in the past. The biggest need, according to most employers and labor market experts, is for workers to have good 'basic' job skills such as basic academic skills, communications skills, adaptability, and the ability to solve problems. While these and other related skills are not technical skills in the traditional sense, they have everything to do with long-term success on the job. And that is what this book is about.

A Different Point of View

You will find references throughout this book to studies by psychologists, sociologists, and labor market professionals. But this is *not* an academic book. Instead, the information forms the basis for a practical and useful handbook for a working person—or one who soon plans to enter the workforce. Many employers asked for such a book to help their new workers succeed on the job. Because of my experience as both employer and trainer of new employees, I believe my perspective can bridge the gap between an employer's and an employee's expectations.

Additional Photocopies

Several pages in this *Instructor's Guide* are one-page worksheets. If you have purchased the *Job Savvy* student text for each student in your classroom, you are authorized to make additional photocopies from this guide to complete any of the activities. You are also allowed to copy the tests.

Ready, Set, Go

You can use this *Instructor's Guide* for high school classes, job training programs, or in the workplace. The exercises, test banks, audiovisual aids, and teaching hints help make the instruction easy and effective. We appreciate your comments and requests for changes in future editions. Please contact us through the publisher listed in the front of this book.

Table of Contents

Introduction

As a supervisor and business owner I have had the opportunity to hire and fire employees. My observations of workers being "let go" confirmed what many employers are currently voicing: Entry-level employees do not always know how to keep their jobs. In other words, an employer can't assume that a new employee "knows the ropes." *Job Savvy* will help reduce the amount of time and money it takes to train new employees in critical areas such as proper dress and hygiene, communications skills, and time management. Employers save money—and employees save jobs.

Job Savvy was written for two reasons:

1. To help employers keep employees on the job. As the workforce shrinks, employers will find fewer skilled workers to do the job. Keeping trained employees will become most important.

2. To help new employees keep—and advance—in their jobs.

In the past, it was often up to parents to prepare their children for the responsibility of their first jobs. One Texan I know related this story about his first job. "My daddy said, 'Son, go down the road to old Mr. Petersen and ask him for a job.'" His father not only told him how and where to get the job, but also checked with Mr. Petersen to make sure that his son did the job properly. In today's society, not too many "old Mr. Petersens" exist. Close contacts with employers are rare and job training is different than in our parents' day.

Problem-Solving Approach

Job Savvy contains ideas for both classroom and workshop instruction as well as individual activities. The case studies and exercises allow students to find solutions to real-life work problems. The basic question is "How do I keep this job?" This *Instructor's Guide* contains suggestions for many additional activities. As the instructor or facilitator, you may choose the activities that fit the time schedule and needs of your group.

Accommodating Students

Job Savvy allows trainees to share personal experiences through group interaction. In general, I suggest that smaller groups are more effective than large groups (over 15 members) and recommend changing the group's members often. This allows more sharing of more ideas.

Dealing with Problem Students

I wish for you a class eagerly awaiting each session. However, realistically, not everyone in a training session will be a "happy camper." Some trainees may resent being required to complete this course. Having a sense of humor will help you deal with these "problem students." If you gain an understanding of why problem students are the way they are, you may view them as individuals needing attention and direction rather than sources of irritation.

General Lack of Interest

If a lack of interest is apparent, let the trainee know you are aware of the problem. In the case of compulsory attendance, your approach may be that if individuals attempt to participate, you will attempt to make the course as rewarding as possible. This is all you can do.

Fear of Formal Schooling

Some trainees may have had unsuccessful experiences in formal school settings. A classroom and instructor could be very threatening to them. Placing chairs in a semi-circle, serving refreshments, and greeting individuals as they arrive will create a less threatening atmosphere. Making yourself available to trainees before, during, and after class sessions will also help break down some barriers.

Shy Personalities

Shy people may suffer from poor self-images, which can be a real threat to learning. Involving a shy person in a small discussion group would be less threatening than a large group discussion. This person needs reassurance. Your facial expressions (smiling or nodding), or short comments like "great" or "good suggestion" can help this individual succeed.

The Dominating Personality

Dealing with dominating individuals is difficult. This person might be insecure. One approach might be to tell the person that others need an opportunity to contribute. If this approach doesn't prove successful, talking privately to the individual might. If this doesn't work, consider asking this person to leave.

Listening is one invaluable skill for an instructor that provides insight into the trainees' needs. It is important to remember that you are in your own unique setting. You judge what approach is best in each particular situation. Use the suggestions that best meet the needs of your group. Be creative and develop your own program that works for you.

Instructor Preparation

Begin your preparation by reading *Job Savvy* and completing the exercises to give you the students' viewpoint. (It will make you a better instructor!) *Job Savvy* encourages lots of classroom participation and discussion. It is a good idea to keep notes in the margin so when one of your students gives you a real gem of an idea, you can use it in a future class.

You are the single most important element in the training session. Be enthusiastic. Your trainees will only be as interested as you are. Be positive. Emphasize the talents of the group. Compliment often. Criticize only if there is no other alternative. Do it privately if at all possible. Remember you, the instructor, are the key to the success of this program!

Planning the First Session

As the instructor, you become your students' employer. Your students should view this class as their place of employment. The way you conduct the class tells your students as much about the world of work as anything you say during the class session.

> **Note:** *The words "student" and "trainee" are used interchangeably throughout this book.*

Getting Prepared

Before you meet your group, here are some things you can do to prepare:

- Plan a class schedule.

- Know your objectives.

- Know your students. (Who are they? What are their backgrounds? Why are they attending?)

- Create a comfortable physical environment.

- Prepare materials and resources.

- Develop a flexible mind-set.

Planning a Class Schedule

A detailed agenda enables you to accomplish the goals you want to reach by the end of each session. Create time slots for each session that will keep slower-paced students moving while keeping the interest of faster-paced students. Of course, this agenda doesn't need to be written in stone. Planning ahead also allows you to prepare for such things as outside speakers and audiovisual presentations.

> **Note:** *If you are working with an individual or small group, it is equally important to plan scheduled progressions. In a small setting, it is even easier to stray from the subject.*

When creating your agenda, it is wise to plan extra activities to use if time permits. Use the "Additional Activities" for this purpose.

Know the Class Objectives

One of the basic objectives of this training is to instill some good work habits in the student. If you use your class as a workplace, you can set and enforce some basic rules such as these:

- **Start on Time:** Expect each trainee to be seated and ready at a set time. You might go so far as having each student "clock in."

- **Student Preparation:** Explain what materials are needed for each session (paper, pencils, pens, etc.). I know of a teacher who requires a shoe from any student needing to borrow a pencil. When the pencil is returned, so is the shoe.

- **Assignment Completion:** Some type of loss or incentive system should help motivate trainees to complete their work.

- **Proper Dress:** Prior to class, instruct students on the dress code. Students should dress in a businesslike manner. If trainees wear uniforms, ensure they know the proper dress and standards.

- **Trainee Conduct:** Set the standards of respect in your class for yourself and the trainees.

You will probably have other objectives for each particular class. Through class participation, the group may help you develop objectives that are important to them.

> ***Note:*** *If you are working with an individual or a small group, each person could make a list of objectives. At the end of the course, review these lists to see what has improved and what needs continued work.*

Know Your Students

Training is far more effective when the instructor clearly understands the student's needs and concerns. Among those items you should try to discover about your students:

■ Why are students attending class? Those who volunteer have different motivations than those required to attend. Adjust your methods accordingly, and use strategies that properly motivate all students.

■ What are your students' personal characteristics? Useful information includes age, gender, ethnic diversity, work experience, and amount of formal education.

■ What are your students' specific training needs? Some students need the most basic job information while others need more advanced information.

■ The more you learn about your students before training begins, the more effective the training will be.

Creating a Comfortable Environment

If you are unfamiliar with the surroundings, arrive early to check out the physical facilities. If possible, allow time to make changes that improve the learning environment. Some environmental influences to consider include:

■ **Room Temperature:** A room that is too hot or too cold may deter learning. As a rule, a little too cool is better than too hot.

■ **Adequate Lighting:** Make sure that lighting is bright enough for reading and taking notes. If your room has a lot of windows, ensure that the sun isn't glaring in anyone's face.

■ **Room Arrangement:** Arrange the chairs in a comfortable way. A semicircle is less formal than traditional rows. (This arrangement would not work in an auditorium.) If you plan on using tables, a horseshoe arrangement allows all participants to see each other while the instructor can move into the middle and talk face-to-face with each participant. If working with an individual, do you want a table or desk between you, or will you sit side by side? Consider how you will feel most comfortable and put the trainee at ease.

■ **Noise Level:** If possible, make sure the room is quiet and free from interruptions. Are the acoustics such that all students can easily hear?

■ **Instructor Placement:** Find a spot in the room to call yours. Where in the room do you feel most comfortable? Arrange the room to focus on this area. Be sure you face the group as you speak and that your back is not toward any individual. You should also take into account where audiovisuals will be shown.

Preparing Materials and Resources

Handouts and training aids should be organized before the class begins. If you have an agenda, it should list what resources you will be using. As a rule, handouts are for the students to keep.

Make sure you are familiar with office machines or equipment you will be using in the classroom. Other materials such as flip charts, transparencies, and videos may require some preparation. Schedule any resource people, videos, and field trips in your agenda also. Do this before the first class session to avoid conflicts later.

Developing a Flexible Mind-Set

Even with all your planning the unexpected will happen, so prepare for the unexpected. It could be positive. It could be a teachable moment. Suddenly something that has been said or done stirs minds. Everyone is alert. Allow this moment to flow. Let the students continue to share. Become a learner rather than an instructor. This doesn't happen often.

Of course, the unexpected could be negative, too. The fire alarm accidentally sounds . . . the electricity goes off . . . the film breaks. Stay calm. Find a solution to the problem and continue with the session.

Beginning the First Session

Introducing Yourself

A simple introduction of yourself is an excellent beginning. Using relevant events from your own experiences will make it more interesting. Include in your introduction:

- Your name

- Relevant facts about your professional or personal life

- A brief description of your first paying job

- Your educational background

- A brief description of your work history

- Your current position

Sharing this information will make you seem more human and establishes communication. Since much of the course work depends on group participation, it is important that you set the example for this communication.

Introducing the Course

A brief description of your purpose and procedures for the course will give trainees an idea of what to expect. Explain rules you will enforce and be specific. If the class begins at 8 a.m, say so. If a break is scheduled, tell the class when and how long. (If a session is more than one hour, a break helps keep interest.)

Be very clear in letting trainees know exactly what is expected of them, and how they will be made accountable for these responsibilities. (Presenting such rules humorously can create a less threatening atmosphere.)

Briefly go over the class agenda. If you expect any special projects to be completed by a particular date, emphasize that. In such a case, establishing dates for various phases of completion a good approach. Thus, the student is encouraged to work on the project throughout the course.

Using word association, ask the class what comes to mind when they hear the word "savvy." Write their ideas on a flip chart or overhead. As a group, summarize the definition of savvy. Now add the term "job savvy." Ask the group to list specific skills that contribute to job savvy in today's workplace. Conclude by pointing out that this course will help each student gain these skills.

Introducing the Group

Divide into groups of four to five people. Ask each group to introduce themselves using the following information:

- Name

- Relevant personal information

- Briefly describe your first paying job

- Briefly describe your *dream* job

- Briefly describe your most recent job

- What you expect to gain from this course?

> **Note:** *If you list the items on a flip chart or overhead, the group can refer to it during this activity.*

Allow two to three minutes per person. Encourage the group to ask questions. With all the groups, have each student introduce another student in their group and tell one thing that was most interesting about the other person.

Exercises like this allow groups to get to know each other in a way that will encourage more class participation. The time spent getting to know one another will help students feel more comfortable sharing ideas later.

In the student workbook, read together the parable at the end of "About This Book." Ask the class to make a list of the possible "mosquitoes" that might cause an employee to lose his or her job. Encourage the group to make the list as detailed and long as possible. Ridiculous answers count!

Conclude the session by explaining any scheduled outside class assignments. Remember to make these assignments meaningful.

Additional Activity: Real People

The following activity exposes students to real people in the real world of work.

Interview two employers or supervisors. A supervisor is any person who gives direction to another person in a job situation. The interview may be done on the telephone or face-to-face. Ask two questions:

1. What changes have taken place in your workplace in the last five years?

2. What are the five most important skills you expect from a successful employee?

Have students record their answers and bring them to the next session.

Additional Activity: Keeping a Journal

This assignment allows students to express themselves and could develop into an on-going course activity.

Ask each individual to keep a "job savvy" journal. The requirement is to write a paragraph or two each day, never more than a page. Ask them to write about their first paying job as their first entry. The following questions may prompt their answers:

- What type of work did you do?

- How did you get the job?

- Who hired you?

- Did you have a supervisor or boss? What do you remember about this person?

- How much pay did you receive?

- How long did you keep the job?

- What factors contributed to your getting (or losing) the job?

Chapter 1

Work Today
. . . and
Tomorrow

The purpose of this chapter is to help trainees understand and deal with the changes occurring in the workplace.

Once upon a time, payday meant making a trip to the local bank, endorsing your payroll check, filling out a deposit slip, then waiting in line for a bank teller to complete your transactions.

Today you may never actually see a bank teller. Your payroll check may be automatically deposited using electronic banking. You can use an ATM to withdraw cash or make deposits. The banking industry is changing.

And banks are not the only workplaces undergoing change. Trainees need to learn to adapt to changing work situations. Being prepared for changes is a matter of survival in today's work world.

Activities

Your Work Experience

Have the trainees read the introduction to *Job Savvy*. Using the information there and the trainees' own work experiences, have the group make a list of the reasons people work.

Before the group completes the exercise "Your Work Experience," briefly discuss the information they'll need, the differences between full- and part-time work, and the kinds of technology that might be used on a job. Ask for an explanation of a temporary agency.

Have the group complete the exercise.

Additional Activity: Tally-Ho

Use the information in the exercise "Your Work Experience" to develop a tally chart showing the group's experiences, under these headings.

Full-time/ Part-time	Company hired/ Temp agency hired	Large company/ Small business

This information may be useful as the group discusses work situations throughout this chapter.

Additional Activity: **Technology and Work**

List the kinds of technology the trainees used in their last three jobs. Discuss how technology changed the jobs.

Additional Activity: **Changes in Technology**

Ask trainees to bring in help-wanted ads from a recent newspaper. Divide the class into small groups. Ask each group to circle occupations that did not exist 30 years ago.

The Labor Force, 2005

Discuss the meaning of the term *labor force*. Have the trainees read this section, then discuss the affect each change could have on them.

1. **The labor force is growing more slowly than before.** Discuss the work situation in your community. Are businesses affected by a slowing growth in the labor force? Are sign-on bonuses offered? What is the age of the average minimum-wage worker in your area?

2. **More women are entering the workforce.** Discuss the number of women working in your community. Ask trainees how many of their mothers or wives work. Is their work full- or part-time? How have women in the workforce affected your community? Discuss services such as daycare and after-school programs. How have businesses in your community responded to women in the workforce?

3. **The labor force is aging.** Are older workers in your community retiring? How are older workers continuing to be part of the workforce?

4. **The workforce is showing greater ethnic diversity.** Discuss the need for ethnic diversity programs. List the various ethnic groups in your community.

Additional Activity: **Making the Choice**

Discuss how each of the following situations could be a positive or a negative experience.

Divide the class into groups of three or four persons. Have each group make a list of positive reactions and negative reactions to each situation.

Case Study 1

Angie, who is 20 years old, is a receptionist at a dental office. Recently Maureen, who is 52, was hired as a second receptionist. Angie has been instructed to train Maureen.

Case Study 2

Carlos and Mohammed work at a local warehouse. Mohammed's religious practices preclude drinking alcohol and eating certain foods. Carlos enjoys going to the local bar with his coworkers at the end of the workday.

What Does Your Workplace Look Like?

Have the trainees complete the exercise "What Does Your Workplace Look Like?"

Ask group members to share their diversity ratings of low, medium, or high. Ask them to share the area of most diversity—age, gender, or ethnic group. If some of the trainees have worked at more than one job, discuss changes from one job to the next.

Organizations and Work

Have the trainees read this section and complete the exercise, "What Kind of Organization Do You Work For?"

Additional Activity: Service or Product

Using the information they gave in "What Kind of Organization Do You Work For?" have the trainees list their jobs as service- or product-producing. Ask them if they work for small businesses (fewer than 1,000 workers) or large businesses.

Additional Activity: Moving Up

Discuss the skills each trainee needs to advance in the workplace. Help the trainees think of ways to use their current skills in a new job situation. Emphasize the importance of updating old skills and developing new ones.

Additional Activity: Video Presentation

Show the video *The Tough New Labor Market and What It Takes to Succeed* (available from JIST).

Occupational Trends

Have the trainees read this section and discuss the table listing earnings and education levels.

Additional Activity: Money, Money

To get a perspective on the difference in salary levels at the various education levels, divide the class into small groups. Ask each group to find out the cost of renting a one-bedroom apartment in your community. They also should estimate a monthly car payment and food and utility costs for a month. Using these figures and the earnings chart, ask each group to figure out how much education is needed to make these monthly payments. Is there any money left over for entertainment and clothes?

Have the group complete the exercise "Thinking About Your Education." Share ideas about keeping their education and skills current.

Additional Activity: Journal Article

Ask trainees to use their current job or a desired occupation as the basis for this exercise. Ask them to write a few paragraphs about the education they'll need to improve their skills and stay up-to-date in this career.

The Structure of Work

Have the trainees read the section and discuss the reasons businesses give for using different kinds of workers. How does keeping the workforce small save money? How does hiring workers for specific projects help a business?

Discuss the three categories of workers and the advantages of each.

- **Core employees** are those hired by an organization to work full-time on an ongoing basis. They usually have benefits like vacation time, holiday pay, and health insurance. Core employees are workers who hold what we traditionally call *permanent jobs*. Core employees often coordinate or lead projects for an organization, and their work is supplemented by subcontractors and temporary employees.

- **Subcontractors** are private business owners—including self-employed individuals—who provide services to an organization. Subcontractors or their employees typically are paid a fee for completion of a task rather than a wage. Their services may be used for a specific project and their work ends when the project is completed.

- **Temporary workers** are those hired by an organization for a short time or whose services are obtained through a temporary employment service. Temporary workers may be hired to work on a specific project, and their employment ends when the project is completed. Temporary workers also are hired when the work load increases beyond the capacity of core employees. Temporary employees often do not have fringe benefits—unless they are provided by the temp service—and their work can be terminated with no advance notice.

Have the trainees discuss these questions:

- What does it mean to be responsible for your career?

- What does it mean to be flexible in your career?

Contingent Workforce

Have the trainees read this sidebar and discuss each type of contingent worker. What are the benefits of being a contingent worker? What are the drawbacks? Who might find this kind of work situation attractive?

Additional Activity: **Journal Activity**

Ask trainees to write a few paragraphs about different ways they can be flexible in their careers. What type of work is attractive to them? What skills would be beneficial in their careers? How would they deal with the sudden termination of a job or project?

Additional Activity: **Guest Speaker**

Invite a self-employed subcontractor and a person from a temporary employment agency to speak to the group about how employees are used in their fields.

Applying What You've Learned

Have the trainees read each case study and answer the questions. Discuss their answers and help them discover what work situations would be satisfying and help them reach their career goals.

Additional Activity: **Supervisor's View**

If you assigned the *Additional Activity: Real People* in the last session, use the first question to summarize workplace changes in your area. Make a list of the changes supervisors have observed. Save the second question to use in the next chapter.

Summing Up

Review Chapter 1 by discussing the changes taking place in the workplace. Use the following discussion questions:

- What changes are taking place in the workforce?

- What changes do you need to make to be successful in today's job market?

- What affect does education have in the workplace?

Chapter 2

Your Employment Relationship

The purposes of this chapter are to help trainees understand the employer's point of view and to learn about employee rights and employer responsibilities.

Starting a new job is a real adventure. Each employee has expectations of what the job will provide.

> My sons took over a newspaper route that had been without a regular carrier for several months. The agreement with the newspaper was that they could keep any overdue bills they could collect. Envisioning large amounts of money accumulating in their bank accounts, the boys were very persistent in their pursuit of the overdue charges. Money was their great expectation. They gave no thought to the fact that their employer wasn't requiring any money for the actual newspapers that had been delivered.

Most employees are like my sons. They expect a job to provide for their satisfaction. They don't consider the employer's expectations. While most employees know that their employer has responsibilities, they are unaware of what those responsibilities are. Often employees have an unrealistic understanding of their employer's expectations.

Activities

What Does My Employer Want, Anyway?

Read the introduction and the sections titled "What Does My Employer Want, Anyway?" and "Workplace Basics" in *Job Savvy*. Allow the students time to complete the "Skills Checklist." Read and discuss the foundation skills and workplace competencies. Discuss the seven basic skills from the ASTD study. Compare their answers to question 2 with those listed in the studies.

Additional Activity: Real People

If the *Additional Activity: Real People* was assigned in the first session, divide the class into groups of four to five people. Each group should select a person to record results. Ask each group member to list the skills expected by the employers and supervisors he or she interviewed. The recorder writes down the skills, keeping a tally of any duplications. (The group decides on duplications.) Allow 10 to 15 minutes for this activity.

Have the groups come together. Each recorder should read his or her group list and tally. Place the consolidated list on a flip chart or overhead. Again, keep a tally of duplications, allowing the class to make these determinations.

Looking over the list, ask the class to point out any expectations that might be unreasonable. Allow free expression of opinions as to the fairness or unfairness of the expectation. No consensus need be drawn.

As a group, find the five most frequently listed skills employers expect. Compare this list with the SCANS study. How do the local employers' expectations compare to the survey? If there is a difference, can it be explained in any way?

Dependability vs. Reliability

Before doing the next two exercises in *Job Savvy,* discuss the difference in meaning of *dependability* and *reliability*. How could a dependable employee be unreliable? How could the opposite be true? Which skill is more valuable: dependability or reliability?

Have each trainee fill in the checklist in this section. Using the checklist, tally the group's opinion, from most important to least important.

Employer Expectations

Have the group read and discuss these three points:

1. Businesses must provide a product or service of high quality.

2. Businesses must satisfy the customer's needs and wants.

3. Businesses must make a profit.

Point out the information in the sidebar titled "Profit."

Now have the group read the section called "Employee Skills." Briefly discuss the 10 self-management skills in the box. Be sure the group understands the meaning of each skill.

Additional Activity: Products and Services

Have the group list the places they have worked. Compile a list of products or services represented. This should provide the group with an idea of the types of businesses in your community. After compiling the list, consider the following questions.

1. What might affect the quality of these products or services?

2. What rules might the employer or supervisor enforce to maintain this quality?

Additional Activity: Make a Profit

To help students understand profit and expenses, divide the class into small groups to work out a solution to the following situation.

> You are in charge of a six-week summer swimming program for preschool children. This is a profit-making venture.

- List all the expenses that might be involved in your business.

- How much will you charge each student?

- What factors other than the expenses you listed may affect your profit?

- How many employees will you have?

- What salaries will you pay them?

Additional Activity: Production Expenses

Have the group form a business making cookies, candy, or peanut butter sandwiches. The group must list all the production expenses. Have them calculate how much of their product must be sold to raise enough money to buy pizza for the entire class. Sell the product. Have the group record sales. If the group makes enough profit, use the money to buy pizza for the entire class.

Additional Activity: Increasing Trainee Awareness

If you are training employees for a particular company, use your company's products or services for this activity.

With the trainees, go through the process of making a product. Together list the expenses the company must incur. Help trainees become aware of the hidden expenses businesses incur. Many employees are totally unaware that expenses such as electricity, insurance, heating, and cooling are part of a business's expenses.

Additional Activity: **Journal Assignment**

Ask the students to choose a self-management skill they could improve and then to write a plan for improving this skill.

Applying What You've Learned

Have the class read the case studies in this section. Ask for volunteers to play the roles of Tom and his supervisor Janet, and of Angel and her supervisor. The rest of the group observes the supervisor's response to each situation. Have the groups complete this statement and then have them explain the reason for reacting this way:

■   If I were the boss, I would have . . .

What Should You Expect?

Have each individual answer the questions. Give the group time to complete their answers.

As a group, list the reasons people work. Post the list for further reference.

Next, list things people like and dislike about their jobs.

Finally, compile a list of employee expectations and wants. Post these lists for reference.

Reasons for Working

Have the group read "Reasons for Working," including the two tables. Compare the reasons workers give for liking their work in these polls with the group's list. Circle the corresponding reasons.

Look at the third table listing external and internal factors of job satisfaction. Briefly discuss what an employee can do to increase his or her job satisfaction. Remind the group that no job is perfect all the time.

Additional Activity: **Video Presentation**

Show the video *Why Work?* with Dean Curtis, a trainer who works with unemployed persons (available from JIST Works). This 15-minute video presents six good reasons for being employed.

Understanding Your Rights

Have students read and complete this section together, including the sections on "Federal Laws," "Fair Wage," "Equal Opportunity," "Child Labor Laws," "Worker Safety," "Labor Relations," "Fair Treatment," and "Working Conditions." This is probably the most complex part of the book, and it is important that employees understand their rights according to the law.

As the instructor, you need to be aware of the laws in your state. Because federal and state laws constantly change, I have provided only a review of these laws here. You must make the decision as to what additional information your group needs. The reference list at the end of Chapter 2 will help you. Local agencies in your area—such as OSHA, the Equal Opportunity Commission, and the State Department of Labor—are another means of information.

Additional Activity: Researching the Laws

Divide the class into small research groups and assign each group a different set of laws to research for class presentation. Provide time for the groups to meet and gather information from the library or other sources. (If library facilities aren't available, you should provide packets of information on each subject to complete this activity.) Using this information and the material in *Job Savvy,* each research group should make a presentation to the entire class.

You could have groups study these topics: fair wage, equal opportunity, child labor laws, worker safety, labor relations, fair treatment, and working conditions.

Additional Activity: Mock Trial

Set up a scene of employer vs. employee, and allow the class to conduct a mock trial. Assign one student to be the judge in charge of the proceedings. The charges should involve misconduct on the part of the employer. (A case involving just cause for dismissal is a good possibility.) The court should include lawyers for both clients, witnesses, and a jury. Other members of the court may be added for interest. Ask the jury to actually bring in a verdict.

Following the trial, discuss the practicality of bringing such actions to court.

Additional Activity: Guest Speaker

Using community resources exposes trainees to the real world. Think about inviting a speaker who works with employee rights issues, such as a union leader or representative, a lawyer, or a local business owner.

Before the person speaks to your group, have the class prepare a list of questions they want to ask.

Resolving Employee Rights Issues

Have the group read this section and discuss the best way to deal with a problem.

Additional Activity: Resolutions to Rights Issues

Divide the class into groups of three or four and have them discuss the following situations. Each group should decide the best way to resolve the problem from the employee's perspective. Share the solutions with the entire group.

The Night Shift

Ty is 15 years old and works in a diner at a 24-hour truck stop. Last Thursday the late-night waitress called in sick at the last minute. Ty's manager asked him to work until 2 A.M. Ty had already worked his regular shift.

Equal Work for Equal Pay?

Mike and Ann began and ended their job training on the same day. They began work on the same day as tellers at the Old Standard Bank. They each work five eight-hour days a week. In fact, they often work at adjoining teller desks.

Today was their first payday. To celebrate, they had lunch together. Over lunch, they compared paychecks. Much to their surprise, Mike's check was $100 more than Ann's.

A Chemical Reaction

Starr works in a photo-processing plant. Recently she developed a rash on her arms. Her doctor says it was caused by a toxic chemical. Starr suspects she came in contact with the chemical in her workplace. She has never received any instructions concerning chemicals in the photo-processing lab.

Sleep on It

Barth has worked at the Sleep Tight Mattress Company for six months. Recently, he expressed an interest in joining Local 82 of the Bed Makers' Union. Today his foreman called him into the office area and pleasantly informed Barth that the company's owner doesn't approve of the union. He suggested Barth seriously reconsider joining.

Applying What You've Learned

Allow time for the group to complete this exercise. Using the two case studies, discuss the fact that all jobs involve both likes and dislikes. These will vary from person to person, because of individual differences.

Additional Activity: Journal Assignment

Have the group write two or three paragraphs using the following opening sentence:

■ "If I believed my boss was treating me unfairly, I would … "

Summing Up

Review Chapter 2 by discussing the three concepts involved in the employer-employee relationship. Questions for discussion include these:

- Why is an employer in business?

- Why do you want to work?

- What do you find satisfying about your work?

- What should the relationship between employer and employee be based upon?

- How is this shown by the employer?

- By the employee?

Chapter 3

Avoiding the New Job Blues

The purpose of this chapter is to acquaint students with what typically happens on the first day at a new job.

First impressions last a long time. So the first day on a job is important to the new worker. Yet because of nervousness and inexperience, new workers often make mistakes that cause real problems.

Remember your first day on a new job? Rolling and tossing in bed the night before? Asking someone if you looked okay as you prepared to leave the house? Looking for a parking place, hoping you wouldn't be late? All this and more awaits your trainees on their first day.

While I can't reserve them a parking space right in front of the building, together we can offer them some information to help prevent embarrassing first-day moments. We'll also cover information on payroll deductions required by the government and various fringe benefits offered by employers. Many new workers have no knowledge of payroll deductions, so their first checks can be a great disappointment.

> **Note:** *The procedures described in this chapter are generally used by companies. If you are training for a particular business, you'll want introduce its procedures here.*

Activities

Reporting to Work

Have the students read the introduction to Chapter 3 and the section titled "Reporting to Work" and discuss the typical first-day activities listed.

Additional Activity: Ice Breaker

Have the trainees complete this sentence.

- "Today is your first day on a new job. Last night you had a nightmare. You dreamed that you arrived at work and you … "

Dress Appropriately

Have students read this section and complete the exercises. Allow time for them to share information on the type of clothing needed in their jobs.

> **Note:** *If you are training for a particular organization, point out the organization's dress requirements.*

If the students don't have jobs yet, assign imaginary jobs to them. Write various jobs on index cards and randomly hand them out.

Starting the Day

Have each student read the sections titled "Starting the Day" and "Paperwork," then fill in the "First Day Checklist" and the "Paperwork Checklist." (Students may use a current or imaginary job when filling in the checklists.) Have them answer as many of the questions as they can. Then, as a group, discuss this information and the possible answers.

> **Note:** *This exercise will give you an idea of your group's understanding of first day procedures.*

Have the students read and discuss the sections titled "Orientation" and "Personnel Information."

Additional Activity: Required Documentation

Ask each student to bring the documents in the "Paperwork Checklist" to class. Look over the documents. Discuss the information the employer would need from each document. Complete the paperwork checklist.

Applying What You've Learned

Give individuals time to read and work through the case studies. As a group, discuss the questions.

Payroll Information and Enrollment

Have the students read the sections titled "Payroll Information and Enrollment," "Withholding Taxes," "Personal Allowances," and "Payroll Information." It's important for trainees to understand this information. Because it is somewhat involved, you may want to discuss it in two parts, with a break in between. Allow time for questions and answers.

Additional Activity: **Reference Groups**

Divide the class into groups of three or four. Assign a different topic to each group. Suggested topics include withholding taxes, payroll information, fringe benefits, required benefits, voluntary deductions, and employee services.

Have the groups collect information on their topics and present it to the entire group.

> **Note:** *Depending on the library facilities available, you may want to compile a file of information on each subject for the groups' reference.*

Applying What You've Learned

Be sure the trainees fill out the W-4 form in this section. Go through it together to make sure everyone understands the format.

Fringe Benefits

Have the students read the sections titled "Fringe Benefits," "Cafeteria Plans," "Paid Time Off," "Required Benefits," and "Voluntary Deductions."

Lead a discussion on the various kinds of fringe benefits. Be sure to point out that not all benefits are available from all employers. Stress the two rules of thumb for choosing fringe benefits.

Discuss the meaning of a cafeteria plan.

Employee Services

Have the students read the section on "Employee Services." Ask them to rank these services in order of importance to them. Is it worth taking a job that pays less but offers tuition assistance? Would you benefit from an employee service such as counseling? The answers will depend on the individual.

Selecting Benefits and Deductions

Have each student complete the first checklist in "Selecting Benefits and Deductions." Divide the class into small groups. In these groups, have each person share why he or she would or wouldn't choose a particular benefit or deduction.

After the discussion, ask the groups to continue with the second checklist. Have each person select the benefits he or she believes are important and share the reasons with the group.

> **Note:** *If you are training for a particular organization, you should point out the fringe benefits the company offers.*

Applying What You've Learned

Have the trainees read the case studies. As a group, list the benefits that each of these individuals needs. Discuss the two situations.

Additional Activity: Guest Speaker

A community resource person can help explain much of this material. Contact a personnel manager, a state or private employment agent, or a company trainer who is willing to speak to your class. To encourage better listening, ask the group to submit questions for the speaker to answer.

Introduction to the Job

Have the group read this entire section (pages 52-54). Discuss the material covered using the following questions.

Work Instructions

- What is your supervisor's responsibility on your first day at work?

- Why is it important to ask questions when instructions are given?

- How can you know what your supervisor expects of you?

Supplies and Equipment

- What would a new worker need to know about supplies and equipment?

- Why is it important to the organization that an employee know the rules about supplies and equipment?

The Phone System

- What might a new worker need to know about the telephone system?

- Why is this skill important to the company?

Breaks

- What does a new worker need to know about breaks?

- What are appropriate reasons for taking breaks?

Additional Activity: **Facility Tour**

If you are training for a particular organization or company, a brief tour of the facility would be appropriate here. Explain the company's policy concerning supplies and equipment, the telephone, and breaks.

Off to a Good Start

Have the students read and discuss the section "Off to a Good Start." Go through the list of suggestions together. Sharing some of your own experiences as a new worker will add a personal touch to the discussion. Emphasize the following important points:

- **Be positive.** New workers often feel ill-at-ease. How can you approach a new job in a positive manner?

- **Ask for help.** New workers need to realize that no question is foolish. Supervisors expect questions.

- **Don't be a know-it-all.** The first few weeks on the job is a time to learn and get to know your coworkers.

- **Have a good sense of humor.** Expect some teasing. As you establish yourself in the group, this treatment should disappear. (Excessive abuse should be reported to the supervisor.)

- **Find a friend.** This should be someone who knows about the job and is willing to help. Not every worker will meet those qualifications.

- **Follow instructions.** You may need to ask questions, but repeating the same questions over and over will irritate a supervisor and make you look foolish. Listen carefully and follow through on instructions.

- **Read company policies.** Supervisors expect their employees to read these policies and ask questions if needed.

> ***Note:*** *If you are training for a particular organization, this is a good time to present the company's policies.*

- **Determine evaluation policies.** Knowing how you will be judged helps avoid surprises at the end of probation.

Applying What You've Learned

Allow time for the students to read the case studies. Divide the class into small groups. Ask each group to share responses to the case studies.

Summing Up

Use the following discussion questions to summarize Chapter 3:

- What can you do to make sure you dress appropriately for your first day of work?

- What benefits are important for you?

- What paperwork will your employer need from you on your first day of work?

- What can you do to make your first day on the job go smoothly?

Chapter 4

Making a Good Impression

The first thing a new worker must do is make a good impression on the job. In this chapter we'll discuss appropriate dress, personal hygiene, and unpleasant mannerisms.

He wore bib overalls and a plaid flannel shirt. His hair was shaggy, his beard long and disheveled. The new car salesman watched him warily for a while. Then, because he didn't have any other customers that afternoon, he finally sauntered over and asked, smiling somewhat smugly, "May I help you today?"

"Well, yes you can. I'll take the black Mercedes convertible in the corner."

The man pulled a thick wad of thousand-dollar bills from his pocket. The cash sale quickly took place … or so goes the tale of the miser from my hometown.

Looks can be deceiving. However, in today's society one's outward appearance does have an effect on the way others treat us. We are judged on our appearance, our personal hygiene, and our mannerisms.

Note: Several of the subjects in this chapter could be sensitive issues, such as body odor, weight, and acne. You must approach these subjects as understandingly as possible. If someone in the group has a special problem, you may want to talk to him or her privately.

Activities

I Haven't a Thing to Wear

Have the group read the introduction and "I Haven't a Thing to Wear" in Chapter 4 of *Job Savvy*. When you introduce this chapter, you should emphasize that the subject is *not* natural beauty. Neatness and appropriate dress make *everyone* more attractive.

Dress Codes

What does it mean if a company has an official dress code? Ask individuals in the group to share their experiences with dress codes, answering the following questions:

■ What kind of clothing did the dress code okay?

▨ What clothing did the dress code rule out?

▨ How was the code enforced?

Be sure the group understands that an official dress code must be fair. It applies to all persons working in that situation. A dress code is a written rule.

> **Note:** *If you are training for a particular organization, you should introduce the company's dress code now.*

What about *unofficial* dress codes? These are the norms of the workplace, the common wisdom that says, even though it's not written down anywhere, we don't wear jeans except on Friday, or whatever. Use the following questions to lead a discussion of dress codes:

▨ How does a new employee learn about the unofficial dress code?

▨ Why is it important to know about an unofficial dress code?

▨ How can an unofficial dress code affect a supervisor's opinion of a worker?

▨ Is an unofficial dress code always fair?

▨ What effect could the unofficial dress code have on one's job advancement?

Appropriate Dress

Don't assume your trainees know what is appropriate dress for different types of jobs. In today's society, people tend to dress for comfort. Younger people are easily influenced by their peers and current styles when choosing their clothes.

Even adults don't always know how to dress. Recently, I was at a patio buffet. The invitation read "cool and casual dress." Clothes actually ranged from shorts and jeans to dresses and heels. Knowing how to dress appropriately isn't always easy.

Be specific when you discuss this topic. Opinions of what is appropriate may vary from region to region. You should have an understanding of what is appropriate in your area.

Additional Activity: Clothes Closet

Bring a suitcase of assorted clothes to class. Take one article of clothing at a time out of the suitcase. Have the students brainstorm what jobs might require this type of clothing. Write their suggestions on a flip chart or overhead projector. Some clothes you might include are jeans, athletic shoes, high heels, a tie, a suit, a sport jacket, a bathing suit, shorts, and work shoes.

Neat Dress

Be sure the group knows that neatness counts in the workplace. For example, torn jeans may be fashionable, but they are inappropriate for most jobs. And some businesses require their employees to wear leather shoes or safety shoes rather than athletic shoes. Wearing comfortable shoes on the job is important for workers.

Additional Activity: Fashion Show

Have each student dress for their job or for the job they intend to have. Some students may dress inappropriately. Discuss what is right or wrong about the way they are dressed for work.

> **Variation:** *Have an occupational dress-up session. Assign a job title to each student. The student must dress for that job.*

Additional Activity: Help from the Pros

Ask a color coordination expert or a home economist to discuss putting together outfits, ways to stretch a wardrobe, and shopping tips.

Uniforms

Have the group come up with a list of jobs that require uniforms. List their ideas on a flip chart or overhead. Why do some businesses require their employees to wear uniforms?

Go through the list of questions in this section as a group, and write down the answers on the flip chart.

Additional Activity: Slide Show

Develop a set of slides showing various uniforms. As you go through the slides, discuss the occupation represented by each uniform. The slides could show people in your own community (for example, a postal worker, an EMT, a police officer, a fast-food server, a waiter or waitress, and a security guard).

> ***Note:*** *If you are training for a particular organization, you should explain the company's policy about uniforms. Answer the questions about uniforms listed in* Job Savvy. *You or someone in the group could model a uniform, showing the proper way to wear it.*

Safety Clothing

Some clothing is worn for protection. Ask the class the following questions:

- Is it a good idea for an assembly-line worker to wear a long chain?

- What would be a good safety precaution for someone with long hair in a job involving machinery?

- Why are steel-toed shoes necessary for some workers? What kinds of jobs require steel-toed shoes?

- In what kind of jobs would leather shoes afford better protection than athletic shoes?

Special Safety Equipment

Have the group read the information on special safety equipment in this section of *Job Savvy.* Go through the list of safety equipment in the book and discuss each item and what it is used for.

Additional Activity: Safety First

Bring in various types of safety equipment. Demonstrate how the equipment is used and why it is needed.

- Place a hard hat on a small pumpkin. Drop a bowling ball or large rock on the hard hat. Now repeat the activity without the hard hat.

■ With a moving machine such as an electric fan, use yarn to show what could happen if hair or a chain were caught in the machine.

> **Note:** *If you are training for a particular company, demonstrate any safety equipment required in your workplace.*

Additional Activity: Guest Speaker

Ask an industrial nurse or a safety expert to talk to the group about safety on the job.

Applying What You've Learned

Allow time for students to do the exercises individually. Then divide the class into groups of three to four. Have the students discuss their selections and the reasons for each choice.

Additional Activity: Journal Assignment

Have each student choose a particular job and write a description of the appropriate kind of dress for it. They should give reasons for the type of clothing they listed.

Personal Grooming

Introduce this section by telling the class that the information in this part of the chapter is private and *will not be shared with the group.* Allow each student time to answer the questions and fill in the checklist in this section.

Additional Activity: Cosmetic Demonstration

Ask a makeup expert or a hairstylist to demonstrate appropriate hairstyles and makeup for the workplace.

Read "A Word About Cologne: Moderation," and discuss the problems cologne or perfume might cause in the workplace.

Special Hygiene Concerns

Have the group read the section titled "Special Hygiene Concerns." As a group, discuss each of the good health practices listed in this section.

> **Note:** *If you are training for a particular organization, you should point out any special hygiene practices necessary for the job.*

Additional Activity: Guest Speaker

Ask a local health department employee to talk about state and local laws concerning hygiene practices in public places.

Special Personal Considerations

Have the group read this section. Discuss each of the conditions and what effect it might have in the workplace. Remember, special sensitivity is called for here.

Additional Activity: Guest Speaker

Any of the following specialists would be a good presenter on these topics: a physical practitioner, a weight-loss expert, a personal trainer, or a dermatologist.

> **Note:** *If you are training for a particular organization and the company has a fitness room available to employees, the group could visit this facility.*

Additional Activity: Physical Fitness

Challenge the students to plan a physical activity program for themselves. It need not be complicated. Simply taking a 30-minute walk each day is a healthy start. Choosing an activity they enjoy is important, because it makes sticking to the program less tedious. Ask the students to engage in a physical activity three times each week. Challenge them to keep up the activity for at least a month.

Mannerisms and Habits

Be sure the group understands what mannerisms are. Go through the list of problem areas. Then ask the group to list other mannerisms and habits people might find annoying. List their ideas on the flip chart or overhead.

Additional Activity: Irritating Mannerisms

Introduce this topic as "a gum-chewing, picking and pulling, slang-using" presenter. Exaggerating these and other mannerisms during your presentation will make the group aware of just how annoying these habits can be. Ask the trainees to demonstrate other annoying mannerisms.

Additional Activity: Journal Assignment

Ask the students to write about irritating mannerisms or speech habits they have. A relative or friend can help them identify one if they can't think of one on their own. Have them write a plan to overcome these habits.

Additional Activity: Guest Speaker

Ask a speech therapist or speech teacher to address the group about developing good speech habits and overcoming speech problems.

Applying What You've Learned

Have the group complete the two case studies. As a class, discuss the questions and the reasons for each answer.

Summing Up

Have the students read the chapter summary. Then ask them to discuss the following questions:

- Why is proper dress in the workplace important to you?

- What effect does good personal hygiene have in the workplace?

- How do mannerisms affect the way you are treated by coworkers?

Chapter 5

Being There
. . .On Time!

Being dependable is important. This chapter presents the problems created by an undependable worker and the effects of absenteeism. A good attendance record is critical in keeping a job, so we'll also cover problems that may cause absenteeism and suggest ways of overcoming these problems.

> **Note:** *You may want to go directly to the activity "Late Arrival" below before introducing this topic.*

Grasping the concept of time is sometimes difficult for the young. My youngest son often asked how long he had to wait before we would leave for a special family outing. Terms like 15 minutes or a half hour meant nothing to him. Finally we solved the time problem by relating it to *Sesame Street:* "We'll go in one *Sesame Street*" made perfect sense to him.

Like my son, many young workers lack an ability to schedule their time. An alarm clock and a calendar aren't parts of their lives. Getting to work on time isn't a high priority. They don't plan ahead for unexpected occurrences.

Activities

Additional Activity: Late Arrival

Arrive for class 5 to 10 minutes late. (This will be most effective if you have been regularly starting the group on time.) Offer all kinds of excuses for your late arrival (flat tire, the cows got out, the alarm didn't go off, your mother called, and on and on).

Ask the group to share their feelings when you didn't arrive on time. What problems, if any, did it cause?

Additional Activity: Problems Caused by Absenteeism

Read the introduction to Chapter 5. Ask the group to define absenteeism and tardiness. Write their definitions on a flip chart or the overhead. Point out that both can cause problems in the workplace.

Additional Activity: Teamwork Game

Divide the class into teams of five or six players. Have each team sit in a circle. Give each group a skein of yarn or a roll of kite string. The object of the game is to roll the yarn or string into a ball. This is a team effort.

At the signal, the first player starts. Play continues by passing the yarn or string to the player on the left. Continue the activity by signaling a player change every 15 to 30 seconds. The first team to form a ball wins.

> **Note:** *Prior to class, make arrangements with a few students to act as "undependable" players. These individuals may leave the group when their turn arrives. They may sit and talk to someone while they are supposed to be working. They may drop the ball or simply stop. At the end of the game, discuss how the other members of the teams felt about these players.*

Additional Activity: Lee and George

Have the students reread the scenario of Lee and George. Divide the class into small groups to discuss the situation. Have the groups consider these questions:

- If you were one of Lee's coworkers, how would you react when Lee returns to work?

- If George ignores the situation, how do you think Lee will react?

- If you were George, how would you handle the situation?

Using the material in *Job Savvy* and the students' own ideas, have the group list problems created by undependable employees. Be sure they list the effects on everyone involved, including:

- The employer

- The supervisor

- Coworkers

- The employee

Be sure to highlight the information in the "Customer Satisfaction" sidebar. Why are dependable workers needed to provide good customer service?

Note: *If you are training for a particular organization, you should present the company's policies on absenteeism and tardiness.*

What's Your Excuse?

Ask each student to fill in the table in this section. Point out that some of the items maybe valid excuses, but solutions are needed to avoid the problems.

Compare their lists with the table in *Job Savvy*.

Additional Activity: No More Excuses

Allow the trainees to share their lists with one other person. Together let them answer these questions:

- How can I solve this problem?

- What is my weakness in this area?

Your Lifestyle Affects Your Work

Have the class discuss each of the areas listed in this section. Some of your trainees may believe these areas aren't their employer's concern. You should encourage them to openly discuss their feelings.

Point out that an employer cannot control an employee's personal life; however, an employer is influenced by some of these items. Consequently a worker's promotions and continued employment may be affected by them.

Additional Activity: Solving Problems

Divide the class into small groups. Using the following worksheet, have each group find a solution to each problem.

When they have completed problems 1 through 4, ask each group to create a problem (number 5) and find a solution. After completing the worksheet, each group should present their original problem to the entire class and challenge the class to find a solution.

Solving Problems Worksheet

1. A mechanic goes home late from work each evening, sits down just long enough to eat dinner, then works on cars at home until he's ready for bed.

2. A worker is so tired she doesn't get her work finished.

3. A worker ignores a customer because he is flirting with a coworker.

4. An employee is late for work with this excuse, "My best friend was arrested in a drug bust last night."

5. Problem: _____

   Solution: _____

   _____

   _____

   _____

   _____

   _____

   _____

   _____

   _____

   _____

   _____

   _____

   _____

Your Lifestyle and Stress

Have each student fill out the stress chart and rate him- or herself.

Additional Activity: Stress Dots

Pass out stress dots to the group. These are small dots that change color to reflect the individual's emotional state. Ask the group to wear the stress dots for a day and keep an hourly record. At each hourly check, they should answer these questions:

■ What color is the stress dot?

■ What am I doing?

> **Note:** For more information write, BioDots International, Inc., P.O. Box 2246, Indianapolis, IN 46206; or call 1-800-272-2340.

Additional Activity: Journal Assignment

Ask the group to write a few paragraphs on something that makes them feel stress, using these questions to guide their writing:

■ Is there a way to avoid this stress?

■ What activity eases my feelings of stress?

Plan for Success

This section lists the five steps to a good attendance record. It's important to go over each step. You should emphasize that these are the steps a worker should take *before an emergency arises*. Read through this section together and discuss each of these areas.

1. **Ensure reliable transportation.** Have the group list the public transportation available in your area. How do you get a taxi? How do you read a bus or subway schedule? Where can you get a rider's pass for the bus or subway?

2. **Make arrangements for reliable dependent care.** Discuss the need for reliable childcare and the problems that can arise if contingency plans aren't made before they're needed. Have the group use the *Yellow Pages* to find childcare centers and health-care programs. Assign trainees to call some of these centers to get the following information:

   ◆ What activities are available?

   ◆ What hours is the center open?

   ◆ Is the center closed for holidays or bad weather?

   ◆ What happens when a child is ill?

   ◆ What arrangements can be made if a child cannot be picked up at the usual time?

3. **Use a calendar.** Have the trainees use the forms in *Job Savvy* to practice using a calendar. The book presents both a weekly and a monthly calendar format. Encourage the group to fill in both business and personal schedules.

4. **Plan a schedule with your supervisor.** As a group, discuss the following questions.

   ◆ How much should a supervisor know about your personal life?

   ◆ Why is it important for a supervisor to know about your personal plans?

   ◆ How much notice should you give before taking a five-day vacation?

   ◆ How much notice is needed for a one-day appointment?

   ◆ Is it possible to take a half day off?

5. **Call the employer.** Discuss the information a supervisor needs when you can't be at work. Who should you talk to if your supervisor isn't there?

> ***Note:*** *If you are training for a particular organization, you should tell the trainees how many absent days in a year are considered reasonable at the company and what disciplinary action is taken when absences are excessive.*

Additional Activity: Guest Speakers

There are several people who could augment this section for you. Below are three suggestions:

- Ask an auto mechanic to share ways to maintain a car for reliable transportation.

- Ask a daycare director to talk about his or her center. Have the group prepare questions before the session.

- Ask a time management expert to speak or show a video on time management.

Notify Your Supervisor

Discuss the following question as a group:

- What is the proper procedure for notifying a supervisor of a delay or absence from work?

Additional Activity: Role Playing

Have the trainees pair up. One student will be the supervisor; the other is the employee, calling to tell the supervisor why he or she can't be at work. You may assign the reasons or have the trainees make them up.

Applying What You've Learned

Have each student fill out the checklist in this section. Go over the list and discuss whether the reasons are good or bad and why.

> ***Note:*** *Highlight the material in the "Friday/Monday Syndrome" sidebar.*

Getting to Work on Time

Read the material in this section and have the group discuss each point. Emphasize again the importance of planning ahead and allowing time for unexpected emergencies.

Additional Activity: Journal Assignment

Ask the students to write a few paragraphs describing something in their lifestyle that prevents them from being a dependable worker. Then have them answer this question:

▪ How can I change my lifestyle to make myself more dependable?

Applying What You've Learned

Give the group time to complete the case studies. Go over the studies and questions together.

Summing Up

Read the chapter summary. Discuss the value of dependability, using these questions to spark discussion:

▪ How will a business benefit by having dependable employees?

▪ How will an employee benefit by having good attendance and being punctual?

Chapter 6

What's It All About?

Learning is a continual process. Trying a new recipe, following directions to a restaurant, and putting together a tricycle are all learning projects. Learning takes place by reading books and magazines, by watching other people, and by sharing information.

Everyone has his or her own unique way of learning. In Chapter 6, we'll look at learning styles and ways of improving job skills to qualify for advancement.

When did you begin learning? At age 5, when you entered kindergarten and learned all you ever really needed to know about life? Of course not! When will your quest for knowledge end? With a bachelor's degree, or a master's degree? Will a Ph.D. complete your learning? Of course not! Learning is a constant, continuing process. Pick up a magazine, turn on the television, watch a demonstration, or talk with a friend and learning will take place.

Many people, however, view learning as a formal, structured activity controlled by others within the confines of a classroom. According to this view, graduation means an end to learning, a task completed.

Activities

Learning Is the Key to Success

Read the chapter introduction and this section. (Don't have trainees complete the exercise yet.) Ask the trainees to define *the learning organization*. What does it mean in the new labor market? Why should the students take charge of their own learning?

Additional Activity: Thinking About Learning

It's important for your students to realize that learning is a continuous activity. Learning takes place throughout your entire life. Employers expect their employees to continue learning on the job.

Discuss the learning that takes place in the first five years of a child's life. Make a list of the basics a child learns. Discuss how this learning takes place. Point out that much of this learning takes place in an unstructured environment, and much of it is done by observing and doing.

Make a list of learning experiences the group has had outside the formal classroom. What skills did they learn? How did they learn them? Who or what served as the "instructor?"

> **Note:** *Some people in your group may believe they are not capable of learning, especially if they have experienced failure in the classroom. These people have a special need for praise in their informal learning. They need to know that this learning is as valuable as classroom learning.*

Have trainees complete the exercise in the section titled "Learning Is the Key to Success," and share their learning project with another student.

Additional Activity: Continued Learning

Divide the class into groups of three or four. Ask each group to make a list detailing what people of different age groups generally know about cars and how they learn about them. What does a child need to know about cars? What learning is necessary for a teenager? What is important for an adult to know? Share ideas together when the groups have completed the task.

Additional Activity: Structured vs. Unstructured Learning

Ask the class to list formal learning institutions. Write their answers on a flip chart or overhead. Now ask them to list informal learning experiences available in your area. Discuss the ways that informal learning might take place in these settings.

Additional Activity: Updating Skills

With the entire group, use brainstorming to come up with a list of all the equipment that might be found in an office. Circle the equipment that would have been found in this same office 20 years ago. Point out the technological changes that have taken place in just two decades.

How Adults Learn

As a group, read and discuss the four characteristics of adult learners. Ask the following questions to spark discussion:

- In what ways do adults learn differently than children?

- Why do adults learn differently than children?

Next, discuss the characteristics of all learners. How can using these learning characteristics help new workers learn to do their jobs?

Learning to Do Your Job

Have the group read and complete the exercise in this section. Discuss the lists they come up with, and their reasons for putting the items on the list.

Where to Find Information

Go through the list in this section together and discuss each item:

■ **Job description:** What is a job description? Make sure trainees understand they may need additional information to get a complete idea of a job's responsibilities.

> *Note: If you are training for a particular organization, go through the company's job descriptions with the trainees. If no job description exists, write one together.*

■ **Training:** Discuss the two types of training that prepare new employees for their jobs. Ask group members to share experiences they have had in their work.

> *Note: If you are training for a particular organization, tell the group what type of training they will receive.*

■ **Supervisors:** Emphasize to trainees that asking supervisors questions is important when information isn't clear. Point out that knowing the evaluation process is important for job security.

> *Note: If you are training for a particular organization, explain the supervisor's role in a new employee's training and evaluation.*

■ **Coworkers:** Point out that observing coworkers should be done wisely. Sometimes a supervisor will team a new worker with a coworker as part of the training process. If, on the other hand, a new worker chooses the coworker, it should be someone who is a reliable worker. Listening to the coworker talk about the job, the supervisor, and other workers is helpful to a new worker; however, the new worker should take caution if the information is overly critical.

- **Friends:** Discuss why is it wise to talk to the supervisor before doing the work the way a friend has suggested.

- **Schools:** List any schools that offer adult and continuing education classes in your area.

> *Note: If you are training for a particular organization, discuss any benefits the company offers to employees who update their skills through additional training. Does the company pay for classes? What are the grade point requirements? What are the requirements for reimbursement? Will additional training result in a pay raise or a promotion?*

- **Conferences:** Discuss any conferences that might be helpful to these trainees.

- **Workshops:** Discuss the ways that workshops vary in quality. Suggest ways to check out workshops and questions to ask about them.

- **Reading:** Discuss the materials available on various occupations. Share any books or magazines you have on this subject. Ask students to do the exercise at the end of the section.

- **Others:** Have the group share any resources they used that aren't a part of the list.

Additional Activity: *What's My Job?*

Divide the group into pairs. Give each pair a specific and different job. No group should tell another group what their job is. Have each group write out its own job description. Go over the following job description with them, so they can use it as a guide. When the activity is complete, have each group read its description. The other groups should try to guess what job is being described.

> *Note: You can list the various jobs on the overhead or a flip chart to make this an easier assignment.*

Sample Job Description

Clerk

Reports to: Project Director

Supervises: No one

Qualifications Desired:

- Minimum typing speed of 55 wpm
- Ability to follow directions closely
- Ability to take shorthand
- Ability to systematically file client records
- Secretarial, receptionist, and/or file clerk experience
- Ability to communicate well and interact with others

Duties and Responsibilities:

- Type all reports
- Type staff correspondence
- Take meeting notes for staff
- Pick up and distribution of projects
- Maintain correspondence, budgets, forms, general files, and other project materials
- Answer telephone and direct calls to proper staff
- Mail outgoing correspondence and packages
- Take phone messages
- Operate office machines as required
- Maintain accurate records
- Update files weekly
- Attend all staff meetings

Your Job Description

Job Title:

Reports to:

Supervises:

Qualifications Desired: _____

_____

_____

_____

_____

_____

_____

_____

Duties and Responsibilities: _____

_____

_____

_____

_____

_____

_____

_____

_____

_____

Additional Activity: Research Continuing Education

Bring in catalogs from schools in your area that offer courses in adult and continuing education. Divide the class into small groups, and give each group a catalog. Give the class a list of various jobs (for example, receptionist, mechanic, nurse's aide, retail salesperson, cook). Have each group list the courses offered at the school that would be helpful for each job.

Additional Activity: Campus Visit

Visit a community college, vocational school, or a school offering continuing education classes in your area. Ask the school counselor to talk to your group about the classes available for adults.

Additional Activity: Guest Speaker

Ask a continuing education or adult education advisor to speak about opportunities to improve job skills in your area. Discuss how the classes are conducted. How much hands-on experience is available?

Additional Activity: Journal Assignment

Have the trainees complete this sentence in their journals:

■ If I were training me to do my new job, I would …

Additional Activity: Software

Introduce your class to the following software (available from JIST Works):

■ *The Electronic Dictionary of Occupational Titles*

■ *The Multimedia Occupational Outlook Handbook*

Spend some time explaining how each software product works and answering questions.

Note: The Dictionary of Occupational Titles *contains almost 13,000 job descriptions compiled by the U.S. Department of Labor. The* Occupational Outlook Handbook *contains detailed information on the largest 250 occupations that employ 85 percent of the workforce. Data on working conditions, nature of the work, job outlook, and educational requirements are among information contained in the OOH.*

Additional Activity: Finding Job Descriptions

Divide the group into research teams of two or three. Give each team a list of various occupations and ask the members to write a job description for each one. They will need to visit the library for this and document their sources.

To add interest to this project, do a little research first and include some unusual occupations in each list.

Learning Organization

What is a learning organization? How does it differ from a traditional workplace? Discuss how a worker contributes to a learning organization.

Applying What You've Learned

Have the group read and do the case studies in this section. Discuss the studies and the solutions the trainees came up with.

Additional Activity: Business Changes

Make a list of the changes that might occur in a business that would require a worker to get additional training.

Education for Life

Not everyone learns at the same pace or in the same way. To learn at their maximum potential, each person needs to know his or her learning style. Although they may not always be able to use their preferred styles, knowing how they learn best will enable your trainees to learn more easily. It also will give them more confidence in their ability to learn. Seeing our learning styles as part of our unique personalities helps us avoid comparing ourselves with others. It helps us accept ourselves.

Ask the group to read through this section and complete the checklist on learning styles. They should rank their three most frequently used methods. Then, as a group, go through the checklist and rank the most frequently used learning methods.

> *Note:* This group ranking may give you some ideas on improving the instruction in this course. For example, if several of your students list observing in their top three learning styles, you might decide to use more videos or demonstrations.

Steps to Learning

Have the group read this section. Go through the learning steps, discussing each one and answering questions as necessary. Ask the students to answer this question:

■ What steps do I need to follow to reach my goal?

Additional Activity: Case Study

Use the following case study to help your students understand the steps to learning. Have the group plan the learning steps Drew needs to take. Write their answers on a flip chart or overhead. Encourage the group to use their imaginations to fill in the resources and reasons for Drew's answers. They will need to "be Drew" for this exercise.

Drew's Learning Project

Drew has worked at the Valley Brook Bank for two years. Recently, the bank manager told Drew that the bank has ordered personal computers for each employee in Drew's department. The computers will arrive in three months. The employees are expected to be proficient on the computers within six months.

Drew has had one computer course at the community college, in addition to a high school course. His friend Kara is a computer store salesperson. Drew is excited about this modernization of his workplace and anxious to get started.

1. What is Drew's motivation? _____

_____

2. When he is done, what does Drew want to accomplish? _____

_____

3. What are Drew's resources? _____

_____

4: What are Drew's best resources? _____

_____

5. When will Drew schedule this project? _____

_____

6. What questions does Drew need to have answered to learn this task? _____

_____

   Who? _____
   What? _____
   Where? _____
   When? _____
   How? _____

7. What can Drew do to ensure he completes the project? _____

_____

8. How can Drew practice what he has learned? _____

_____

9. How can Drew evaluate progress on his learning project? _____

_____

Personal Learning Project

This exercise is designed to help trainees plan individual learning projects. Give trainees sufficient time to fill out the questionnaire and to share learning projects. Encourage them to follow through on their plans.

Applying What You've Learned

Divide the class into small groups. Have the group read and do the case studies. Use the questions in the section titled "Personal Learning Project" as a guide in planning. Allow time for each group to complete its project. Then review the case studies together and record the group's responses. The format might be like this:

- **Skill desired:**

- **Person's motivation:**

- **Possible resources:**

- **Best resources:**

- **Time schedule:**

- **Progress evaluation:**

- **Practice skill:**

Review Activity: Job Savvy Video

The video *You've Got a Job, Now What?* provides a good review of Chapters 1 through 6 of *Job Savvy*. (The video is available from JIST Works.)

Summing Up

Read the chapter summary. Use the following questions to emphasize the importance of continued learning.

- What types of learning can you use to gain new skills?

- Why is continued learning important to an employee?

- Why is it important to your employer that you continue to learn?

Chapter 7

Knowing Yourself

In this chapter, trainees will use a skills checklist to discover hidden skills they have that are valued in the workplace. Throughout the chapter, trainees are encouraged to view themselves in a positive way. Despite what others may say, each of us is responsible for forming our own positive or negative feelings about ourselves.

Blind, deaf, and unable to speak, the child's world was limited to the fenced yard of her home. Yet she grew to be a world traveler, a speaker, and a writer. Helen Keller became so well-known that a major motion picture told her story.

Growing up poor and black, and raised by a single parent, Dr. Ben Carson is now recognized worldwide as a gifted neurosurgeon. He led the first surgical team to successfully separate Siamese twins joined at the head. Yet when he began practicing at Johns Hopkins University Medical Center, nurses and patients often mistook him for an orderly.

What makes some people succeed despite hindrances in their lives? What makes others fail despite their talents? In his book *Gifted Hands,* Dr. Carson contends that our inability to *think big* often prevents us from achieving our greatest successes in life.

You really can't think big unless you have a positive self-concept. In the workplace, employers look for people with confidence. Such employees are more motivated on the job. They are more creative in their work. These are traits employers want in their employees.

Activities

Your Self-Concept Can Make You or Break You

Have the students read the first section of Chapter 7. Discuss the terms *self-concept*, *self-image*, and *self-esteem*. Why is an employee with self-confidence more valuable to an employer?

Discuss the "outside influences" on a person's self-concept. Point out that those influences can be both positive and negative.

Additional Activity: Personal Influences

To illustrate outside influences, ask the trainees to draw their personal circles of influence. They should draw themselves in the middle of their circle, then place around themselves the people (family, friends, coworkers), organizations (churches, schools, clubs), resources, (money, cars, homes), or activities (hobbies, athletics, interests) that influence how they feel about themselves.

Discuss self-awareness, using these starter questions:

- What is self-awareness?

- Why is it important to know your skills?

- How will knowing yourself affect your self-concept?

Additional Activity: **This Is Me**

Ask each trainee to create a word picture of him- or herself using a list of descriptive nouns. To get them started, demonstrate by describing yourself. For example, here is my word picture:

Verne is a

- Trekie

- husband

- writer

- father

- bookworm

- stamp collector

- junk food junkie

- football fan

After each individual has completed his or her list, divide the class into pairs and let the partners share discoveries. You may want to have them trade partners and continue sharing one or two more times.

> **Note.** *If you are working in a one-to-one situation, make a list yourself and share it with the trainee.*

Applying What You've Learned

Allow time for the students to read and do the case studies. Discuss each study and the answers they came up with.

Note: If you are working in a one-to-one situation, point out the reasons this trainee was hired for his or her position. Discuss the skills he or she possesses that got him or her the job.

Learn to Believe in Yourself

Have the class read the section titled "Learn to Believe in Yourself." As a group, make a list of circumstances that might affect someone's self-concept in a negative way. Some examples are divorce, a poor grade, loosing a job, being rejected by a friend, and being criticized. Use the following questions to spark discussion:

- How is your self-awareness important when you are facing negative circumstances?

- What effect can your self-awareness have on your work relationships?

Additional Activity: Guest Speaker

Check with a local mental health association for information on forming a good self-concept. If the association has a speaker's bureau, ask if it can provide a speaker to address your group on ways to improve self-concept.

Additional Activity: Journal Assignment

Have students use the following fantasy as the basis of a journal article.

You have been granted one special wish: You may change anything about yourself that you want.

- Write about what you will change.

- Write about what you will keep the same.

Take Control of Your Life

Note: Before starting this section, explain to the trainees that "Your Approach to Life Quiz" is private. It is intended for their own use. Scores will not be revealed in class.

Allow time for each trainee to complete the quiz titled "Your Approach to Life." Explain the scoring method and allow time for scoring. Go through the scoring interpretation. Allow each person to interpret his or her own score.

Learn to View Life Positively

Have the trainees read this section. Point out that even people with poor self-concepts can learn to believe in themselves. How can a person develop a positive attitude toward life? Each person must take credit for his or her successes. And each person should analyze his or her failures to find their causes. Discuss the tips listed in the box titled "Selling Yourself on You." How can these tips improve your self-image?

Personal Evaluation Exercise

Note: *This exercise may be difficult for some people to complete, especially those lacking self-confidence. Encourage everyone in your group to complete the exercise. Point out the need to look for everyday successes—not just monumental ones.*

Allow enough time for each individual to complete this exercise. Then divide the group into pairs and let the partners share their responses. (You may want to let individuals choose their own partners, since some items might be personal.)

Self-Concept in the Workplace

Allow time for the trainees to read this section. Use the following statements and questions to spark discussion:

1. **You will make mistakes.**

   ◆ How should you react when you make a mistake?

   ◆ What's the best way to react to criticism from your supervisor?

71

2. Your employer wants you to succeed.

◆ Why do you think your employer hired you?

◆ How should you react to compliments from your supervisor?

Additional Activity: Flatter Yourself, Please

Divide the group into pairs. Have each partner write a note complimenting the other person. When the writers are finished, ask them to read their notes to their partners. After each person has written and read his or her notes, discuss the feelings this exercise produced. Have the students answer these questions:

▨ Was it easier to write the compliment or to read it to the other person?

▨ How did you feel when you were complimented?

▨ Was it easier to compliment or be complimented?

▨ What is the value of a compliment?

Identify Your Skills

Use this section to emphasize your trainees' individual skills. Knowing their skills will add to their self-awareness. Point out that skills are divided into the three areas listed in *Job Savvy*.

Self-Management Skills

What are self-management skills? These are the skills basic to keeping a job. Many of these skills are reflected in the way a person approaches his or her personal life. Some of these skills are personality traits. Others have to do with getting along with others and adapting to various job situations. Go through the list of skills in the checklist. Be sure the group understands the meaning of each skill. Why would an employer value each skill? Explain how to score the checklist. Give the group time to check and score the checklist.

Transferable Skills

What are transferable skills? These skills are used in more than one job. They are important for getting promotions and raises. Go through the checklist. Be sure the group understands the meaning of each skill. Emphasize that the skills are listed under various headings describing their usefulness in the workplace. Give the group time to complete and score the checklist.

Job-Related Skills

What are job-related skills? These skills have been developed through life experiences. Because they reflect personal interests, these are the skills used in jobs that are particularly attractive to a person. Allow time for each trainee to fill in the job-related skills section. Point out the method used to score the section.

A Review of Your Skills

Allow time for the group to read this section. Have the trainees record the scores from each of the skills areas. Ask the following questions:

- Why is knowing your skills your strongest point as an employee?

- Did you discover a skill you weren't aware you had or one you haven't been using?

- Did you find a weak skill? How can you improve this skill?

Allow time for the students to write short statements expressing their feelings after identifying their skills.

Applying What You've Learned

Divide the class into small groups. Have the members discuss the case studies and answer the questions.

Summing Up

Discuss the tips listed here for improving self-concept. A healthier self-image takes time and work, but it is possible with a positive outlook on life. Challenge each trainee in your group to think of one success he or she has had during this *Job Savvy* experience. How will your students reward themselves for their successes?

Getting Along with Your Supervisor

In this chapter, the trainee has the opportunity to view the workplace from a supervisor's perspective.

Dagwood had Mr. Dithers. Fred Flintstone had Mr. Slade. Lois Lane had Perry White. On or off the job, everyone has a boss, but not everyone wants to admit it.

In today's society, many young people grow up without authority figures who serve as role models. This means that many young employees enter the workforce not knowing "who's the boss." This leads to problems—problems that can result in dismissal. Many entry-level employees have no idea what responsibilities their supervisor has. They may, in fact, view the supervisor's job as easy. From their point of view, the supervisor stands back and bosses while the other employees do the "real work." The supervisor may even be viewed as the "enemy," constantly looking over each worker's shoulder, watching for mistakes.

It's vital for trainees to understand the importance of having a good relationship with the supervisor. They need to know that their supervisor plays an important role in their success and happiness on the job. The supervisor often has great influence in such matters as promotions, salary increases, and employee dismissal.

Activities

Introduction

Have the students read the introduction to Chapter 8. Discuss the definition of supervision. Point out that cooperation between supervisors and workers is critical to the success of any business.

Additional Activity: Supervisor Definition

Divide the class into groups of three or four. Ask each group to define the word *supervision* and list the responsibilities of a supervisor. When they have finished, have each group share their definition and list with the rest of the class. Write a class definition and list on a flip chart or overhead.

The Team Leader

Have the class read this section of *Job Savvy*. Look at the various titles given to supervisors: leader, coach, cheerleader, teacher, and counselor. Discuss these titles as they relate to a supervisor's work

Now read the box titled "Delegate" together. Discuss the meaning of the word *delegate*. Ask trainees the following questions:

▪ Why is delegating necessary?

▪ What problems can result when a supervisor delegates work?

▪ What problems can result if a supervisor doesn't delegate work?

▪ Who is responsible for the problems that result in each situation?

Additional Activity: Trust Walk

This activity illustrates the trust involved in delegating tasks. Ask each person to find a partner. One will be the leader; the other the follower.

> **Note:** *No one should be forced to participate in this activity. Give an opportunity to "sit this one out" if anyone is reluctant to take part.*

No talking is allowed during the trust walk. On signal from the instructor, the follower, with eyes closed or blindfolded, is guided through a designated area by the leader. The walk should last at least five minutes. When the walk is completed, ask about the feelings each person experienced. Use the following questions for discussion starters:

▪ How did the followers feel?

▪ Did anyone open his or her eyes during the walk? Why?

▪ How did the leaders feel?

▪ Was there a temptation to talk to the follower rather than to guide him or her?

▪ Why?

Now apply these feelings to a supervisor who is trusting a new employee to do a task

What Does a Supervisor Do?

Allow time for the trainees to complete the exercise individually. Divide the class into small groups and ask group members to compare their ratings and the reasons for these ratings. Ask each group to make a list of responsibilities they believe the supervisor cannot delegate. Compile these group lists into one class list of responsibilities the supervisor cannot delegate. Discuss the following questions:

- Why can't these jobs be delegated?

- Are there any jobs that the supervisor would never do?

It's Not an Easy Job

Read this section together as a class. Discuss the following question:

- How can an employee understand a supervisor's responsibilities in the workplace?

Good "Followership"

Have the students read this section. Go through the list together and discuss how each principle would help in the workplace.

Communicate with Your Supervisor

Briefly point out the five essentials for good communication with a supervisor.

Now go through the list step-by-step, discussing the problems that might be encountered as instructions are given on the job.

Emphasize that listening carefully and asking questions are important, but a supervisor should be given the opportunity to give the information before questions are asked. Repeatedly asking the same question might annoy a supervisor.

> **Note:** *If you are training for a particular organization, use this time to demonstrate any task a new trainee may need to learn.*

Additional Activity: Nonverbal Communication

What do people mean when they talk about *body language* or *voice inflections?* Make a list of these kinds of communication. What do they indicate to an employee? Demonstrate the effect of pointing to an object, raising an eyebrow, whispering, frowning, waving one's hands, stepping back from a person, raising one's voice, and placing one's hands on one's hips. What messages do these actions convey?

Additional Activity: Video Presentation

Have the class view a short teaching or demonstration video on any subject *with the audio turned off.* Ask the students to make a list of all the nonverbal communications they observe.

Now show the video with the sound on. Did the students get the import? Could they understand what was being taught without the words? Did they make any mistakes?

Additional Activity: Follow Directions

Ask a resource person to visit the classroom to demonstrate a local craft. After the demonstration, allow the group to make the craft following the demonstrator's directions.

Jargon

Read the box titled "Jargon." Although learning a new "language" may be difficult, it is a part of the job. Emphasize that trainees should ask questions if they don't understand what is meant by a particular term.

Additional Activity: Word Game

To illustrate the different uses of words, write the phrase "a vehicle with four wheels" on the flip chart or overhead. Ask the group to brainstorm a list of other words that could suggest a vehicle with four wheels. Write their ideas on the flip chart. Point out how each word meets the definition but has a different meaning.

> **Note:** *If you are training for a particular organization, explain any jargon commonly used in that business.*

Understand Instructions

Have the students close their books. Give each a blank sheet of paper. Read the four-step directions under "Understand Instructions," one step at a time. *Don't repeat the directions.*

Now have the trainees open their books, read the section, and do the exercise under "Understand Instructions." Allow time to discuss their answers to the question.

Ask Questions

Have the class read this section and discuss the three points. Ask the following questions:

■ Why is asking right away important?

■ How does summarizing responses help supervisors?

■ What if the supervisor isn't available?

■ Why is memorization important?

■ If you have problems memorizing, how can you keep from repeating questions?

■ How does summarizing responses help workers?

Additional Activity: Learning to Ask Questions

The following case studies will teach trainees how to phrase questions for their supervisors. In each case a problem has occurred in the workplace and the supervisor is presenting the problem to the employee or employees. Using the old newspaper questions (who? what? where? when? why? and how?), have the trainees find the information given by the supervisor. If information isn't given to answer one of the questions, have the group form a question that will elicit the information they need.

Fast Eats at The Eatery

Nelson, the headwaiter at *The Eatery*, is holding a meeting of all the serving personnel before the evening shift begins. Here's what he has to say:

"Last night several customers complained that the back dining room wasn't being served quickly. Complaints ranged from cold food to lack of refills on coffee. There was a team of three on duty back there, but since that area has been designated as the nonsmoking section, more diners are asking to eat there. So, I'm putting two more people on the crew for this evening's dinner hour. Let's go now, it's time to get on the floor."

- What is the problem?

- Where did the problem occur?

- Who will be involved in solving the problem?

- How will the problem be solved?

- What question would you ask if Nelson was your supervisor?

Moving Patients

Mary is the head nurse in the hospital maternity ward. One of the new mothers has developed an infection. Mary is holding a briefing at shift change. Here's what she has to say:

"Mrs. Johnson has a staph infection, and she can't remain in the maternity area of the hospital. Josh and Suzanne, I'll need your help."

- What is the problem?

- When did the problem occur?

- Where did the problem occur?

- Who will be involved in solving the problem?

- How will the problem be solved?

- What question would you ask if Mary was your supervisor?

Report the Results

Read this section together and discuss each point. Emphasize the need for employees to take responsibility for developing communication with their supervisors.

Additional Activity: Scenes from the Workplace

Divide the class into groups of three to role-play the situations below. One person plays the supervisor, one plays the employee, and the third acts as observer. The observer should point out any clear or unclear communication between the supervisor and the employee.

> **Note:** *Give each group a copy of these scenes. Have the members of the group change roles after each scene is completed.*

Scene 1

The supervisor asks the employee to restock the toppings in the ice cream bar. The employee has completed the job.

Scene 2

The supervisor tells the employee to make 15 copies of a memo. The memo is addressed to all employees. The employee knows there are 25 people in the office.

Scene 3

The supervisor places the employee in the appliance section of the store. The employee has never worked in appliances. A customer wants to know which refrigerator is more energy efficient.

Coaching Your Job Performance

Have the class read this section and discuss the importance of listening to the supervisor about one's job performance. Point out that some of this communication will be informal: For example, the supervisor might give words of encouragement or demonstrate an easier way to get a job done. Some job performance communication is more formal: For example, the supervisor might ask you to have a private discussion or review a performance evaluation form. Whatever the form of communication, there are some points trainees should remember:

- **Don't respond to feedback with anger.** Sometimes feedback from a supervisor is negative. Discuss the best way to handle negative feedback, ways to handle emotions in such situations, and appropriate responses if supervisors shout.

- **Know what it is you have done wrong.** Remind trainees to ask questions. If the supervisor is angry, the employee should calmly apologize and ask how to do a better job the next time.

- **Thank your supervisor for compliments.** Point out that a simple "thank you" lets the supervisor know his or her attention is appreciated. No one enjoys being ignored when they give a compliment.

- **Ask for feedback.** What if a supervisor is a "clam?" Point out that asking for feedback about work habits is a good idea. It shows job interest.

Additional Activity: Criticism Evaluation Self-Test

This exercise lets trainees test their personal reactions to criticism. No one can do everything the right way every time. At some time in our work experience, we all receive criticism. This quiz shows trainees the areas where they need to improve so they can use criticism in a positive way.

Criticism Self-Test

Instructions: *Mark the items listed with "yes" or "no." Be honest. This quiz will give you an idea of how well you accept criticism. It will help you see ways you can improve your attitude and behavior when you are criticized.*

Yes **No**

☐ ☐ Do you avoid your supervisor when you make mistakes?

☐ ☐ Do you get angry when your supervisor criticizes you?

☐ ☐ Do you use other employees' poor work as an excuse for yours?

☐ ☐ Do you give excuses for your mistakes?

☐ ☐ Do you avoid admitting that you made a mistake?

☐ ☐ Do you feel personally attacked when you are criticized by your supervisor?

☐ ☐ Do you need to defend yourself when you are criticized?

☐ ☐ Do you need to talk back to your supervisor?

☐ ☐ Do you need to prove you are right and your supervisor is wrong?

☐ ☐ Do you sulk after you have been criticized?

☐ ☐ Do you talk to coworkers about your supervisor's criticism?

☐ ☐ Do you always believe your supervisor's criticism is unfair?

☐ ☐ Do you criticize your supervisor after he or she criticizes you?

☐ ☐ Do you continue to think about the criticism for a long time afterward?

☐ ☐ Do you shout back at your supervisor if he or she shouts?

☐ ☐ Do you criticize your supervisor behind his or her back?

☐ ☐ Do you think about quitting when you are criticized?

☐ ☐ Do you ignore your supervisor's criticism?

Scoring the Criticism Self-Test

For each question, "no" is the preferred answer. Award 5 points for each "yes." Use the following table to evaluate your use of criticism.

20 points or below: You accept criticism very well.

20-30 points: You accept criticism satisfactorily.

30-40 points: You accept criticism fairly well.

Over 40 points: You need to work on this skill.

Performance Appraisal

Read the box "Performance Appraisal" out loud. Discuss what might happen during a performance appraisal with a supervisor. If you can get some sample forms used in evaluations, share them with the group.

> **Note:** *If you are training for a particular organization, discuss the evaluation process used for new employees in that company.*

Applying What You've Learned

Allow time for individuals to record their answers for each case study. Discuss the case studies and their answers with the group.

Meet Your Supervisor's Expectations

Read and discuss the introduction to this section. Emphasize that supervisors typically are involved with many workers. Their problems are multiplied when several workers break "little" rules.

> **Note:** *Don't assume that the trainees know how to practice these six behaviors. Although this may seem like basic knowledge, many new workers have lost jobs because they didn't practice one of them. Take the time to read and discuss each point.*

85

List each of the six behaviors as the group discusses it. Make sure the trainees understand what each point means and how it should be practiced. Emphasize the importance of each point. *Be specific.* Have the trainees answer the questions under each point.

Applying What You've Learned

Divide the class into small groups. Using the case studies, ask each group to answer the questions. Review each group's conclusions.

Resolving Problems

Sometimes problems arise between supervisors and employees. People don't always agree. The trainees need to know how to communicate respectfully with their supervisors when disagreements occur.

Introduce this section by reading the following definitions:

- **Conflict resolution** means talking to your supervisor about the disagreement. You or your supervisor may initiate this.

- **Grievance procedures** involve filing a formal complaint about the disagreement. Usually, you will fill out forms for this. Other people (such as a personnel director or a chief executive officer) may be involved. Sometimes, a union representative guides the employee throughout the process. The employee initiates this procedure.

- **Disciplinary action** occurs when your supervisor is unhappy with your job performance. This is a formal procedure set up by the company. It varies from company to company. Your supervisor initiates this procedure.

Conflict Resolution

Allow time for the group to read this section. Go through the six suggestions for solving conflicts. Discuss each point.

Grievance Procedures

Allow time for the group to read this section. Discuss the seriousness and complications of grievance procedures. Note that filing a formal grievance will cause stress between an employee and a supervisor. Point out that in some cases this is a necessary step; however, it should only be taken with much forethought.

Note: If you are training for a particular organization, explain the grievance procedures used by the company.

Disciplinary Action

Allow time for the group to read this section. Discuss the four disciplinary steps and explain each.

Note that an oral warning is the first step. If he or she takes the warning seriously, an employee should be able to correct the problem without any further discipline. Employers seldom want to fire workers unless it is absolutely necessary.

At times an employee should look for another job. When might it be wise for an employee to look for another job?

Note: If you are training for a particular organization, be sure to discuss the disciplinary policies of the business.

Additional Activity: Language Resolution

Using the six guidelines listed under "Conflict Resolution," have the trainees restate the following negative statements in a way that helps solve the conflict rather than cause more problems.

1. You never told me to fill the ice tubs. How was I supposed to know?

2. If I can't have this weekend off, I'm quitting.

3. Sometime when you have a chance, could you and I talk about this problem I'm having?

4. You give me fewer hours than any of the other people who work here.

5. You ordered too many copies of this book and now you expect me to sell them. Forget it! It's your mistake.

6. You should have told me sooner. Thursday night is my bowling league. I can't work late.

7. So I jammed up the copier. It's not like you never made a mistake.

8. I know what I know. Mary Alice told Troy, who told me just what you said about my not getting that promotion.

9. Well, you can't fool me. I heard there's going to be a big layoff next month.

10. You're always in the back room when the evening rush starts.

Additional Activity: Guest Speaker

Invite a union representative to explain his or her part in dealing with the grievance procedure.

Summing Up

Read the section titled "Summing Up." Important discussion questions include these:

- ▓ Why is it important for an employee to maintain a healthy relationship with his or her supervisor?

- ▓ What if a supervisor and an employee disagree?

Chapter 9

Getting Along with Other Workers

In this chapter, you'll show your students how to be effective team players, and why that's important. The need for tolerance in the workplace is a hot topic these days because of the increasing diversity of the workforce. Trainees must be able to find solutions to conflicts with coworkers.

When my sons were little, one of my greatest summer pleasures was watching their T-ball games. In T-ball, players are assigned field positions, just like in baseball, but the pitcher doesn't pitch. Instead, batters hit the ball off a rubber post, called the tee. No one sits on the bench in a T-ball game; everybody plays. Since there often are 15 to 20 kids on a team, the outfield has lots of coverage. Occasionally, a real slugger enters the batter's box. With one fierce swing, he or she sends the ball into the outfield. The outfield goes wild, each child trying desperately to grab the ball from the other. That's when you suddenly realize your child isn't a team player.

Teamwork is important. On the playing field, a sports team that can't work together doesn't win. In the laboratory, a team of scientists achieves more if they share ideas. Even at home, sharing household duties gets the job done faster, allowing leisure time for everyone.

In the workplace, teamwork has become common in recent years. Managers and supervisors have been trained to organize workers into teams. They view themselves as team leaders, and they expect each person to cooperate in achieving the same goal. It's vital that trainees understand the importance of getting along with other workers.

Activities

Additional Activity: Introducing the Team Concept
Introduce the chapter by discussing the following questions:

- What is a team?

- Why are teams used in the workplace?

- How does the teamwork approach affect a supervisor's perception of his or her workers?

- How does the teamwork approach affect the relationships between coworkers?

Additional Activity: **Tinker Toys**

Divide the group into work teams of four people. Place a Tinker Toy sculpture on a table. Allow the group to observe the sculpture for one minute, then cover it with a box.

Give each group just enough Tinker Toys to create the same sculpture. Their job is to recreate the sculpture using all of the pieces. Emphasize that this is a team effort. Allow the groups time to complete their sculptures. Uncover the original sculpture for comparison.

> **Note:** *Privately ask one member of each team to observe the other team members as they complete this task.*

Using the following questions, the observers should record their impressions of how the group handled this problem.

- Was there a group leader? Who was it?

- Was there disagreement in the group?

- How was this disagreement approached?

- How did the group react to the leader?

- If there was no leader, how did the group organize to solve the problem?

- Would assigning a leader help the team work better?

Discuss the information each observer collects.

Get to Know Your Coworkers

Ask the trainees to read the introduction to this section and complete the exercise. Then go through the list together, discussing why each person chose "yes" or "no."

There may be some disagreement, since not everyone will view the situations in quite the same way.

How You Fit In

Read this section together and use the following questions for group discussion.

Know your position

■ Why is it important to know what other workers expect?

■ Can anyone in the group relate a work situation that involves team members doing a task in a particular way?

■ Why might a new worker be expected to do the "dirty work," such as cleaning up at the end of the day?

■ Why should a new worker do this type of task?

Accept good-natured teasing

■ Why do coworkers tease and play jokes on new workers?

■ What is the best reaction to such joking?

■ If the teasing becomes a problem, why would it be wise to talk to the coworkers first rather than going to the supervisor?

■ What is the difference between joking and harassment?

> **Note:** *Harassment and discrimination will be discussed further later in this chapter.*

Do your fair share

■ Describe a situation in which someone doesn't do their part of a task. How does the group react to the situation? How do they feel about that person?

■ Describe a situation in which someone does the entire task rather than let others help. How does the group react to the situation? How do they feel toward that person?

■ When is it wisest to do what the supervisor says?

Don't do other people's work

▓ Why is it unwise to do other people's work?

▓ Is it ever wise to help someone else with his or her work?

▓ What should you do if you have completed all of your work and there is still time in the workday?

▓ If you have completed all of your work, is it all right to do someone else's work?

Know how your team functions within the organization

▓ Why is it important to understand how other teams affect your work?

▓ Who is responsible for problems that develop between teams within the organization?

> **Note:** *Emphasize that becoming part of the team takes time. Point out that both the established team and the new worker are adjusting to the situation. If new workers remain calm and accept their positions, this process will go more smooth.*

Synergy

To introduce the phenomenon of synergy, have the class read the box, then divide the participants into two groups. Explain that each group will be manufacturing paper chains. You will need to supply glue and precut paper strips (½" by 4¼") for each participant.

Instruct the first group to form teams of three. Give the teams time to plan how they will perform this task.

While they are planning, explain to the second group that they will work alone. They are not to communicate with each other in any way.

Allow the two groups to begin working at the same time. After 5 or 10 minutes, stop the workers. Compare the work of the two groups. The teams of three should have produced longer chains.

Applying What You've Learned

Allow time for the group to do this exercise. Discuss the two case studies.

The Value of Diversity

Read the introduction to this section together. Divide the group into two teams. Have the students list five characteristics that make them unique. This can include things they can do, a personality trait, a hereditary characteristic, and so on. Have them sign the paper. Collect papers from each person, keeping the two teams' papers separate.

Pick a paper and read the characteristics to the opposite team. This team has three guesses to identify the person. Score 3 points if they are correct on the first guess, 2 on the second guess, and 1 on the third. Continue play in the same manner with the opposing team.

When you have read all the papers, total the teams' scores.

Additional Activity: Let Me Count the Ways

Brainstorm a list of all the ways that people in any given work situation may differ.

Values

What is meant by *personal values*? Give some examples of personal values. Discuss how these values are formed. Give an example of how people with differing values might strengthen a work team.

Read and discuss each of the three general personality categories and the values associated with each. Have the group read and follow the instruction in the values exercise in this section.

Additional Activity: Categories

This activity can be used for discussion in a large- or small-group situation. It also can be used as a handout exercise for individuals.

Categories Worksheet

Using the three general categories (traditionalist, humanist, and pragmatist) decide which type of person might have made each of the statements below. Place a **T** (traditionalist), **H** (humanist), or **P** (pragmatist) in front of each statement.

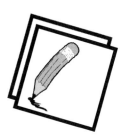

_____   I'm not working this weekend. I deserve a rest.

_____   I'm expecting a promotion to assistant manager by next June.

_____   That's the way my boss taught me to do it, so that's how I do it.

_____   I'm working next Saturday because the boss asked me to.

_____   My boss called me in today. She congratulated me on getting the Thompson account finalized. I hope she is thinking of a raise.

_____   I'm asking for next Saturday off. I have a hot date with Stan.

_____   The manager was out of town today and I practically ran the office myself. I'm signing up for the account course the company is offering next month.

_____   My company is opening a childcare center for its workers. That's really progressive for it.

_____   I plan to stay with my company till I retire.

Additional Activity: Value Comparison

Divide the class into groups of three or four. Have groups list the values they have on the following issues. Then have the groups compare values. Encourage students to discuss what they believe influenced their values.

- Paid vacations

- Company family outings

- Company-paid education

- Working overtime

- Changing jobs

- Getting a promotion

- Merit pay raises

Effective Work Teams Blend Values

Read these two paragraphs. Discuss the need to have all types of people in a work team.

Find out how many people fit into each personality/value category. Ask each student to share his or her reasons for deciding which category fits. Point out that no value system is totally good or bad.

Temperaments

Have the class read this section and discuss each of the temperament types. Then have the students complete the exercise.

Additional Activity: Temperamental Journey

Consider each of the temperament types. What type of temperament might choose each of these occupations?

- Inventor

- Judge

- Scientist

- Soldier

- Cartoonist

- Teacher

- Police Officer

- Radio Disc Jockey

- Baseball Player

- Artist

Dealing with Different Temperaments

Read this section together and discuss how to approach conflicting temperaments.

Additional Activity: Temperaments Unite

Ask the group to divide themselves into temperament groups. Ask each group how they would react to the following problem. What would their solution be? Compare each group's reactions and solutions. Would the different reactions and solutions cause conflicts?

A woman in your workplace is causing problems. Although she has never attacked anyone physically, if there is a disagreement with other workers, Jody's behavior often is very aggressive. Your supervisor has talked to Jody, but her bullying continues. Last week a new worker was so frightened that he resigned. Jody works at an acceptable pace and your supervisor indicates that he will not fire her. The grapevine says that Jody is having problems at home too.

■ How did your temperament group react to this problem?

■ How did your temperament group solve this problem?

■ How could differing temperaments affect the solution to this problem?

Individual Diversity

Allow time for the students to read this section. Ask the questions below to stimulate discussion.

Gender

1. Read this statement from *Job Savvy:*

   Women often are more attentive to the needs of other people, while men tend to be more aggressive and ambitious.

2. How would this diversity strengthen a team in each of the following workplaces?

   ◆ A used car dealership

   ◆ A walk-in medical clinic

   ◆ A computer store

Ethnicity

1. Read this statement from *Job Savvy:*

   Oriental cultures traditionally value cooperation, while Western cultures emphasize individualism.

2. How would this diversity strengthen a team in each of the following workplaces?

   ◆ A hair salon

   ◆ An elegant supper club

   ◆ An auto repair shop

Age

1. Read this statement from *Job Savvy:*

    Younger workers typically bring enthusiasm and energy into a job. Older workers bring patience, maturity, and experience.

2. How would this diversity strengthen a team in each of the following workplaces?

    ◆ A hardware store

    ◆ A floral shop

    ◆ A bakery

Additional Activity: Journal Assignment

Have the students write a few paragraphs using these starter sentences:

■ I have a biased view about working with …

■ I formed this bias because of …

■ I could overcome this bias by …

Additional Activity: Is a Disability Always Visible?

To help trainees become aware of various types of handicaps, brainstorm a list of disabilities. Remember to include "unseen" disabilities, such as diabetes, dyslexia, mental retardation, and epilepsy. Encourage anyone who has had an experience with a disabled person to share with the group.

> **Note:** *If there is a person with a disability in your group, encourage that person to share his or her views and experiences.*

Additional Activity: Attitude Check

Use the following quiz to help your students examine their attitudes toward disabled people. Although the students shouldn't be required to reveal their answers, you may want to discuss each statement and examine the reason people might have for their attitude.

Check Your Attitudes Worksheet

Directions: *Mark each statement below true or false. Be honest.*

_____ 1. Disabled people feel sorry for themselves.

_____ 2. Mentally challenged people are always happy.

_____ 3. Blind people can't hear well.

_____ 4. Disabled people expect special treatment in the workplace.

_____ 5. A disabled person can't be a contributing member of a work team.

_____ 6. Mentally challenged people are sexually over-stimulated.

_____ 7. Epilepsy is contagious.

_____ 8. Disabled people need someone else to handle their financial decisions.

_____ 9. The mentally challenged can't live independently.

_____ 10. Deaf people can't communicate intelligently with hearing people.

Scoring Your Attitude Check

The right answer in this quiz is always "false." Have the students score 1 point for each correct answer. Using the following scoring system, have them rate their attitude toward disabled individuals:

10 Points: Excellent attitude

8-9 Points: Good attitude

7-6 Points: Need to improve

5-0 Points: Poor attitude; need education

Encourage your students to get to know disabled individuals to broaden their perceptions. Disabled people are individuals, and should be treated as such.

Additional Activity: Guest Speaker

Check with a local speaker's bureau for any group or individual who could share information about disabilities with the group. Sources for information on the disabled include local mental health associations, the education department of a local hospital, or social service agencies in your area.

Some disabled individuals might be willing to share their experiences with a group. This would give your class a terrific opportunity to realize that, although disabilities affect real people, *the disability isn't the person.*

Other good sources of information are local businesses. Ask a representative of a business that hires disabled employees to relate the company's experience.

Basic Human Relations

Read this section as a class and discuss the 14 steps listed.

Divide the class into groups of three or four. Give each group a copy of the following exercise.

Basic Human Relations Worksheet

Directions: Using the 14 steps listed in this section, write the step number that offers the best reaction to each situation.

_____ 1. You walk into the break room and overhear Pam and Rich talking about Nick's latest romantic antics.

_____ 2. Jane has asked you to join the company volleyball team.

_____ 3. You are upset because Ryan has been taking materials from your desk rather than getting his own supplies from the storage room.

_____ 4. Your supervisor says you need to speed up and get more work completed during the day. You've tried, but you aren't sure how to go about it.

_____ 5. At 9:30, Marcia asks if you are ready for a break. Pablo and Sy are going for a cup of coffee.

_____ 6. Last week when you were sick and missed a day of work, Jon typed up your report, which was due that day.

_____ 7. Lonnie believes Nanette isn't doing her share of the work. He wants you to talk to the manager about it.

_____ 8. You like your new job, but you really miss your old friends at your former job.

_____ 9. Yesterday Luke put the wrong toppings on a customer's pizza and had to make a new pizza. The customer was upset at having to wait so long for the order.

_____ 10. All the servers in the ice cream shop have to put together their own ice cream orders. At your former job, one person put together the sundaes and other ice cream orders. You think that system worked a lot more smoothly than this one.

Applying What You've Learned

Discuss the ways that one can react positively and negatively. Emphasize that a positive approach offers reassurance and support to fellow workers, while a negative approach creates uneasiness and even ill feelings between coworkers.

Divide the class into small groups. Have the groups discuss each case study, answering the questions listed in the book. Then have each group share its conclusions as the class discusses each case study.

Good Electronic Manners

Read this section and discuss each guideline. Emphasize that e-mail, faxes, voice mail, and computer information should be private. Trainees need to realize that other workers (and the supervisor) may have access to any messages or information sent electronically.

Special Problems with Coworkers

Read the following sections together and discuss the issues and how they affect the workplace. The questions listed under each heading are designed to increase awareness about these sensitive issues.

Sexual Harassment

- What types of conduct or behavior can be interpreted as sexual harassment?

- Can either gender be guilty of sexual harassment?

- Does sexual harassment involve only members of the opposite sex?

- Could the way you dress be interpreted as a type of sexual harassment?

- Could certain phrases be interpreted as a type of sexual harassment?

- Why might an employer consider firing you for sexual harassment?

103

    ■ Sexual harassment charges don't always surface at the time of the incident. Why does this happen? What effect does this have on the parties involved?

    ■ What should you do if you are the victim of sexual harassment?

Note: Point out that filing a sexual harassment charge is a very serious step that could affect a person's employment and reputation.

Racial Harassment

■ What types of behavior could be interpreted as racial harassment?

■ Is racial harassment usually the result of ignorance?

■ One of your coworkers is telling racial jokes. How should you handle this situation?

■ One of your coworkers constantly uses an offensive racial slur when referring to another worker. How should you handle the situation?

■ What should you do if you are the victim of racial harassment?

Note: Again, point out the need to take such an accus-ation very seriously because of the damage it can cause.

Dating

■ Why is dating a coworker a real possibility for many people?

■ When could dating a coworker become sexual harassment?

■ Why do some companies have a "no dating" policy? Does your company have such a policy?

■ How can dating a coworker cause problems in the workplace?

■ You are dating a coworker. What can you do to avoid situations that will cause conflict?

Violence in the Workplace

Read this section as a class and discuss ways that violence can be avoided. Talk about ways to protect yourself in the workplace.

Summing Up

Read the chapter summary and answer the questions below:

- Why is teamwork so important in the workplace?

- In what ways are people different?

- How can differences make a work team stronger?

Chapter 10

Meeting the Customer's Expectations

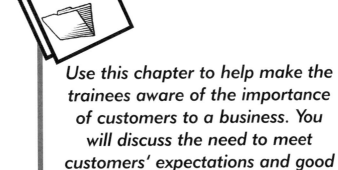

Use this chapter to help make the trainees aware of the importance of customers to a business. You will discuss the need to meet customers' expectations and good customer service.

> The man at the back table is signaling for a refill on his coffee. The toddler at table 5 just spilled her milk. And a whole busload of teenagers just headed for the remaining tables in your section. Satisfying customers is not an easy job. In fact, customers can be a real pain. But customers are necessary if a business is going to be successful.

It's important for trainees to understand the need for good customer service. They must realize that businesses must have customers to make a profit and to remain in business. Businesses without customers simply do not exist.

Activities

The Customer Is Always Right

Have the trainees read the introduction and first section of Chapter 10. Discuss the importance of customers to a business or to any organization.

What does the term *customer service* mean? Discuss the chart in this section. In many businesses, who influences customers the most? What about an employee might influence a customer?

What Is Good Customer Service?

Have the students read this section and complete the checklist. Discuss the trainees' experiences with good and poor customer service. Did these experiences affect whether they returned to the business?

Additional Activity: Journal Article

Using the definition of good customer service in *Job Savvy*, ask trainees to write a few paragraphs on how they expect to be treated as customers.

Providing Good Customer Service

Read the section "Providing Good Customer Service." When does the act of customer relations begin? Why is making a good first impression with a customer important? Discuss the three ways that your actions affect customers.

Additional Activity: Contrasting Situations

Discuss a customer's reactions to the different situations using these four questions:

1. How will the customer treat you?

2. How will this affect the customer's choice in buying the product or service?

3. How will this affect the customer's opinion of the company?

4. Who or what is the difference in each situation?

Have the students contrast the two situations. Discuss the difference between the two situations.

Situation 1

You work in the office of a lawn care service. A customer calls to subscribe to the service. The telephone rings 12 times before you answer it. You put the customer on hold. After a minute, you greet the customer.

Situation 2

The next day a customer calls to subscribe to the lawn service. The telephone rings two times before you answer it. You put the customer on hold. After a minute, you greet the customer.

Situation 1

You work in the sales department of a mail-order company. Your company guarantees delivery in two days. A customer faxes an order for 100 copies of a book listed in the company's current catalog. Only 50 copies of the book are available. You send the 50 copies and put the others on back order.

109

Situation 2

Another customer faxes an order for 100 copies of a different book. You send 100 copies of that book to the customer. The books arrive in two days.

Have a Good Attitude

Read this section. Discuss the need to make customers the top priority in the workplace.

Make two lists using the headings **Nuisance** and **Necessity**. Under **Nuisance**, brainstorm a list of ways customers can cause interruptions in completing a job. Under **Necessity**, brainstorm a list of ways customers are important to the worker.

Make the Customer Feel Good

Read this section and answer these questions:

- What is meant by giving a customer a hug?

- How can you make a customer feel important?

- What is meant by "making a customer a raving fan?"

Greet Customers

Read this section. Use the following questions to spark class discussion:

- Why is it important to greet customers?

- What should you do if a second customer comes into your work area while you are helping another customer?

- What should you do if a customer enters your work area while you are finishing your job?

■   What should you do if a customer enters your work area while you are on the phone with another customer?

Additional Activity: Role-Play

Use the following role-play situations to involve the trainees in greeting customers. Give different trainees the roles of customers and workers in each situation.

Situation 1

You work in a sporting goods store. Cal is shopping for a baseball glove. You have been helping him for about 5 minutes when Lorna comes into the store. She is looking for a pair of inline skates.

Situation 2

You work in the office of a cable TV company. You are on the phone with Mike, who is having trouble with his cable channels. Rosalind comes into the office to pay her monthly bill.

Listen to the Customer

Have the class read this section. Discuss ways workers can be sure the customer's needs are made clear. Discuss the five steps listed.

Now discuss the ways body language can say "I'm listening" or "I'm not listening." On the flip chart or overhead, make lists of listening/not listening body language.

Additional Activity: Understand the Customer's Need

Talk about the difference between open-ended and closed-ended questions. Why do open-ended questions work best for finding out what a customer wants? Change the following closed-ended questions to open-ended questions.

111

1. Are you looking for brown shoes?

2. Are you purchasing a compact car?

3. Are you putting this lamp in the living room?

4. Are you having coffee?

5. Do you want pepperoni?

Take Action

Have the students read this section. Use the following questions to spark discussion:

■ What can you do in your job to exceed the customers' expectations?

■ Why is it important to exceed a customer's expectations?

■ What results might a business see if workers are giving customers extra service?

Additional Activity: Satisfy the Customers' Needs

Divide the class into groups of three or four. Ask each group to write a short skit involving customers and employees serving the public. They can choose any type of organization, from a drug store to a social service agency. They may include both poor and good service. They may even create props and costumes. Allow time for the groups to plan their skits during the session.

Have each group present its skit to the entire class. Ask the other groups to list the types of good and poor service they observe during the skits. Was any extra service given? How did customers react?

Applying What You've Learned

Give trainees time to work through each case study. Discuss each study and the answers in each situation.

Basic Customer Needs

Read the tip in the box. Discuss the meaning of each of the six basic customer needs. Use the example in *Job Savvy* to help your students understand practical ways to meet these customer needs.

Additional Activity: **Journal Assignment**

Ask your students to patronize three different businesses in your area. Have them record their reactions, both positive and negative, as "customers." What did an employee do to cause their reaction?

Good Customer Service on the Telephone

Read this section as a group. Brainstorm the many ways businesses use the telephone. Discuss the importance of the telephone to business.

Answer the Phone Promptly

Read this section and discuss the meaning of the "three-ring policy." Why do some businesses have such a policy?

Additional Activity: **Prompt Answering**

Discover how to answer the phone quickly in each situation.

Situation 1

You are showing a customer a video camera. The telephone rings. How do you handle this situation?

Situation 2

You are typing a business letter that your boss needs in the next 10 minutes. The telephone rings. What should you do?

Situation 3

You are checking out a customer. The telephone rings. How do you handle this situation?

Situation 4

You are talking to a customer on the telephone. The second telephone line rings. What do you do?

Proper Greetings

Read this section as a group and answer the following questions:

- What information should you give a customer when you answer the phone?

- If the telephone call is transferred to you, what information should you give?

Additional Activity: Greetings Role-Play

Assign students to role-play each of the following situations. The goal for each worker is to answer the telephone giving the needed information in a clear, organized way.

Situation 1

You work for Blazer University Library in the reference area. The main switchboard has transferred this call to the reference desk.

Situation 2

You are the receptionist at WQYZ AM, 1120, The Listener's Station.

Situation 3

You are taking pizza delivery orders at Lorenzo's Pizzeria.

> ### Situation 4
>
> You work in the service department at Byte Computers. The receptionist has transferred this call to your department.

Listen to the Customer

Read this section as a group. Use these questions to spark discussion:

- Why is it more difficult to understand a customer's needs over the telephone?

- What should you do when you understand what the customer wants?

Take Action

Read this section as a group. Discuss the problems you may have explaining the actions you are taking to a telephone customer.

Additional Activity: What Will You Do?

Have the students role-play the following situations. You may take the role of the customer. The student should take the role of the employee. The employee needs to explain the steps that will be taken to solve the customer's problem.

> ### Situation 1
>
> You work for Banker's Credit Card. A customer calls needing a copy of last month's billing. Explain to the customer what you will do.

> ### Situation 2
>
> You work for Anne's Mail-Order Service. A customer calls to say that she was sent blue towels. She ordered white towels. Explain to the customer what you will do.

Situation 3

You work for Stuart's Fashionable Men. A customer calls to say that he did not receive the sale price on the suit he purchased yesterday. Explain to the customer what you will do.

Situation 4

You work for Money Bank. A customer calls to say that a deposit made last week is not recorded in her checking account. Explain to the customer what you will do.

Putting a Customer on Hold

Read this section as a group. Use the following questions to spark discussion:

- What should you do before you put a customer on hold?

- What are some of the negative factors of putting a customer on hold?

Additional Activity: Role-Play

Have trainees role-play the following scenes. One person should be the telephone customer and one should be the worker. A second customer in the business could be introduced.

Scene 1

You work in a video store. A customer has called asking if the store has a copy of *How to Survive on the Job*. You need to check the store's inventory.

Scene 2

You are a receptionist in a styling salon. You are on the phone dealing with a customer who is having problems rescheduling an appointment. The second line has rung four times.

Scene 3

You work in a clothing store. A customer calls wanting to know if the store still has a size 44 plaid sports coat he saw last weekend. The sports coats are on the other side of the store.

Transferring a Call

Read this section as a group. Ask the following questions:

- What are the steps to follow when transferring a call?

- Why might a customer be irritated when a call is transferred?

Additional Activity: Sticky Situations

Discuss what should be said or not said in the following situations.

Situation 1

You have been away from work due to illness. Barb, your supervisor, took your place while you were out. You have been back at work 10 minutes when an unhappy customer calls. She says that Barb overcharged her. The customer needs to talk with Barb, but Barb is not coming in today.

117

Situation 2

A caller asks a question you cannot answer. You suggest that he talk to your supervisor. When you transfer the call, you find that the supervisor is at lunch.

Taking a Message

Read this section as a group and discuss the steps for taking messages.

Now divide the trainees into small groups. Each group should discuss each situation below and tell what should and should not be done.

Situation 1

Your supervisor is at lunch with a business contact. A customer calls asking to speak to your supervisor. The caller wants your supervisor to call her back as soon as possible.

Situation 2

A coworker is out of the store due to a family problem. She plans to be back to work in two days. A customer calls and insists that he will only talk to her. He wants to know why she is not working.

Situation 3

Your coworker is showing a customer a new car. Another customer calls, asking for her. He has decided to buy the car he looked at last night. He wants to set up an appointment with her as soon as possible.

Applying What You've Learned

Working individually or in small groups, have the trainees read each case study and fill in the information. Discuss the results as a class.

Dealing with Difficult Customers

Read this section together. Start a discussion about difficult customers by answering the following questions:

- What types of complaints might customers have? (Think of your own experiences as a customer.)

- What might cause customers to be angry?

- What might cause a customer to be rude?

Customer Complaints

Read this section. Discuss why customers may complain by answering the following questions:

- What problems in the company may cause customer complaints?

- What customer complaints may be caused by the customer?

- What problems involving a third party may cause customer complaints?

Use the following questions to discuss ways to resolve a customer complaint.

- What must you do before you can solve a customer's problem?

- How would you handle a complaining customer who is disturbing other customers?

- How can you find out what to do to satisfy a customer with a complaint if you do not understand the problem?

- What should you do if you can not do what the customer is requesting?

■ Why is it important to let the customer know what action has been taken to solve the problem?

Additional Activities: Guest Speaker

Ask a person who works in the customer service department of a local business to address the group. Have the class prepare questions in advance. Here are some examples:

■ How do you handle angry customers?

■ What is the most common complaint you hear from customers?

■ What is your company's policy for dealing with customer complaints?

■ What was your most difficult customer service experience? How did you handle it?

Angry Customers

Have the class read this section. Explain to students that a customer's anger should not be taken personally. Here are some other discussion questions:

■ Why do customers become angry?

■ How can you calm an angry customer?

  – Stay calm yourself

  – Let the customer know you realize he or she is angry

  – Tell the customer you can help solve the problem if they calmly explain it to you

■ What should you do if a customer refuses to become calm?

Additional Activity: Calming Anger

Use the following situations to discuss ways to calm an angry customer. Your students should finish each dialogue by adding the employee's response.

Dialogue 1

Customer: Waiter, this is not the meal I ordered. Can't you get anything straight? I want my food in the next five minutes or I'm leaving.

Dialogue 2

Customer: I want you to know that I am not a happy customer. Your company is a bunch of liars. Your floor wax does not work and my brand new kitchen floor is ruined. I am going to report you to the Better Business Bureau.

Dialogue 3

Customer: What kind of business are you running here? Your dry cleaning ruined by daughter's prom dress. What are you going to do about this? I want to see the manager. Now! Do you understand?!

Dialogue 4

Customer: What do you mean my video is overdue? I am not going to pay a fine. What kind of a fool do you think I am? You're just trying to make more money off me. Well, I'm not going to give you another penny.

Customer Rudeness

Read this section as a group. Use the following questions for discussion:

- What examples can you give where customers were rude to an employee?
- What causes customers to be rude?
- What are some effective ways to handle rudeness?

121

Applying What You've Learned

Have the trainees work individually or in small groups to read the case studies and answer the questions. Let them share their ideas with the whole group.

> **Note:** *For additional information on communication, show the video* The Art of Effective Communication. *It deals with listening skills, verbal and nonverbal communication, and proper telephone use. This video, based on the book* Effective Communication Skills, *is available from JIST Works.*

Review Activity: Working 9 to 5 Video

The video *Working 9 to 5* provides a good review of Chapters 7 through 10 of *Job Savvy*. (The video is available from JIST Works.)

Summing Up

Read the chapter summary and review the chapter using the following questions:

▦ Why is customer service so important to a business?

▦ How is customer service important to government and nonprofit agencies?

▦ What are some ways to meet customers' needs?

Chapter 11

Problem-Solving Skills

This chapter highlights the reasons employers are looking for workers with problem-solving skills and introduces a variety of ways to approach problems. Trainees are encouraged to practice these problem-solving skills using their own creativity.

Real simple, right? Climb out of the car. Lock the door. Rush into the restaurant. The waiter directs me to the dining room. No problem! I've arrived just in time for the staff luncheon. But wait … where are my car keys? Could it be?

Life is complicated and full of problems. Just when you least expect it, you need to call on your problem-solving skills again.

The workplace is no exception to this rule. As organizations become ever-more complicated, there is a greater need for workers who can solve problems. Workers with problem-solving skills are valued by employers. Trainees need to understand that problem solving is a highly marketable skill.

Activities

Management Through Team Work

Read the introduction, the section titled "Management Through Team Work," and the sidebar on "Total Quality Management Teams." Discuss this material using the questions below as a guide.

- What is meant by the term *employee involvement?*

- What is a quality circle?

- As an employee, would your attitude toward your job change if you were a part of a quality circle? How?

- Why are employees becoming more involved in problem solving?

Additional Activity: Video Presentation
Show one of the following videos (available from JIST Works):

- *Learning to Solve Problems.* This video shows the steps to take in problem solving.

- *How to Problem Solve: Critical Thinking Skills.* This addresses objectives identified by the *SCANS Report for America 2000.*

Problem Solving

Have the class read this section and discuss the three basic assumptions, answering these questions:

- Why is it important to believe that a problem can be solved?

- What is meant by this statement: "Often, it is only possible to find probable causes"?

- In what way is problem solving a continuous process?

The Problem-Solving Process

To prepare for this discussion, have each person read this section. Lead the group through the seven steps to solving problems. List and discuss each of the steps.

Note: The following exercises may be used to give the students more experience with analyzing data. Since this information isn't available in Job Savvy, *you have permission to make copies for the trainees.*

Data Analysis

The second step in the problem-solving process is gathering and analyzing data. There are three simple methods for analyzing data. This exercise will show how frequency tables, percentages, and graphs are used to analyze data.

Frequency Tables

There are two types of frequency tables. One table is used for data collection and the other for data summary.

Data Collection Frequency Table

The frequency table for data collection has three columns. The left column is labeled *Item*; the middle column, *Tally*; and the right column, *Number*. A description of the observation or answer is written under *Item* each time something different occurs or a new answer is given. A mark is made in the *Tally* column beside it. This process continues until all observations or data have been recorded. Count the number of marks in the *Tally* column and record the total in the *Number* column.

Table 1 is a sample frequency table with data on customer complaints about lawn mowers.

Table 1. Data Collection Frequency Table

Item	Tally	Number
Motor quits working	⁤₊₊₊₊	5
Handle breaks	₊₊₊₊ ₊₊₊₊ 1111	14
Starter won't work	111	3
Oil leaks	₊₊₊₊ ₊₊₊₊ 1	11
Blade falls off	₊₊₊₊ 11	7
Tires fall off	1111	4
Controls won't work	₊₊₊₊ 1	6
		50 Total

The frequency table provides information at a glance. In Table 1, for example, one can easily see the problem that occurs most frequently: "handle breaks." The problem that occurs the least: "starter won't work." This table also provides maximum (14) and minimum (3) numbers. The difference between the maximum and the minimum numbers is called the *range*. In Table 1, the range is 11.

Percentages

Percentage can be defined as a fraction with a denominator of 100. The percent sign (%) is substituted for the decimal in the fraction. Thus, 83% could be expressed as 83/100. Percentages help compare items.

Since percentages have the common denominator of 100, they can be added, subtracted, multiplied, and divided. For example, if 25% of a store's customers buy something on Friday and 28% buy on Saturday, you can say that 53% of all sales are made on Friday and Saturday.

Percentages for frequency tables are calculated by dividing the number of observations of one item by the total number of observations, then multiplying by 100. Below is the formula to figure percentages.

$$\frac{\text{One Item}}{\text{Total}} \times 100 = \text{Percentage (\%)}$$

Table 1 showed that 14 customers reported broken handles. The total in the *Number* column is 50 customer complaints. Place these numbers in the formula like so:

$$\frac{14}{50} = 0.28 \times 100 = 28\%$$

Using this example, you could say that 28% of all customer complaints are due to broken handles. Percentages provide the information necessary to complete a data summary frequency table, such as Table 2.

Table 2. Data Summary Frequency Table

Item	Number	Percent(%)
Motor quits working	5	10
Handle breaks	14	28
Starter won't work	3	6
Oil leaks	11	22
Blade falls off	7	14
Tires fall off	4	8
Controls won't work	6	12

Using percentages, it is possible to find the most frequent reasons for customer complaints and add them together. Using the Table 2, then, we can say that 50% of all customer complaints are because of handle breaks (28%) and oil leaks (22%).

Pareto's 20/80 Rule

An interesting discovery made by a man named Vilfredo Pareto was *that there is a disproportionate distribution that seems to exist in many areas of business and economics*. This disproportionate distribution is often called

127

Pareto's 20/80 rule. (A specific application is referred to as the *ABC Inventory Analysis.*[1]) For example, 20% of an organization's inventory accounts for 80% of the sales; 20% of customers account for 80% of all sales; 20% of manufacturing mistakes account for 80% of product defects. In solving problems, it often is true that 20% of people, things, or processes cause 70% to 80% of a problem.

Graphs

Another way to organize data is to use graphs. Graphs help the eye visualize the data and draw conclusions. There are several types of graphs. The exercise below illustrates the *bar graph*.

Bar graphs compare quantities. They work well for displaying data in frequency tables. The bars allow you to compare items listed in the table. The following bar graph displays the data in Table 1, illustrating which complaints are made most frequently. Looking at the graph, it's easy to see which complaints occur most often.

To create a graph, one must understand its different parts. Look at Figure 1 for reference as you follow the steps to draw your own bar graph.

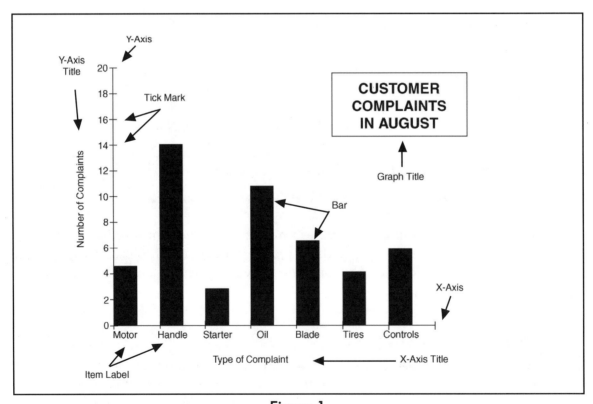

Figure 1

Create the X-Axis

The X-axis is the horizontal line on the chart. In business charts, the X-axis usually is a person, place, event, or time period. In other words, the X-axis isn't used to display numbers.

1. Count the number of items to be displayed on the X-axis. (There are seven items in the sample.)

2. Draw a horizontal line 6 inches long about 1½ inches from the bottom of the paper. (A standard sheet of paper is 8½ inches by 11 inches, so a 6-inch line allows a 1¼-inch border on each side of the chart.)

3. To calculate the distance between each mark on the X-axis line, divide 6 inches by the number of items to be plotted plus 2. (Adding 2 to the number of items provides space between the first mark and the Y-axis. An equal amount of space is reserved on the right side of the X-axis line.) This is calculated for the sample chart like this:

$$2 + 7 = 9 - 6'' \div 9'' = \frac{6''}{9} = \frac{2''}{3}.$$

4. Draw the marks plotted for each item on the X-axis line. Use the distance calculated in Step 3 to measure the space between each mark. For the sample chart this was done by measuring 2/3 inch from the left side of the X-axis line and making a mark. This is where the first item was plotted. Every 2/3 inch, another mark was drawn, until all seven marks for the X-axis were drawn.

5. Label the marks on the X-axis using a one-word description for each item plotted. Write the description under the marks. In the sample chart the labels are Motor, Handle, Starter, Oil, Blade, Tires, and Controls.

Create the Y-Axis

The Y-axis is the vertical line on the chart. In business charts, this typically is a range of numbers. The Y-axis is used to find the value for each item on the X-axis. This value is marked or plotted to correspond with the values on the X-axis.

The number at the bottom of the Y-axis typically is zero. Follow the steps listed to create the Y-axis.

1. Draw an 8-inch vertical line starting at the left point of the X-axis line.

2. Calculate the range of numbers to be used to determine the scale for the Y-axis marks. Take the highest value for the plotted items and round to the highest number divisible by 10, 100, 1,000, and so on, depending on the values of the items on the X-axis. For example, the highest value in the sample chart is 14, so the highest rounded number of the range is 20.

3. Divide the highest number in the range by the number you want to use for increments of each mark. The sample chart uses increments of 2. Be creative in deciding what increments to use so your chart displays data in a way that is easily understood.

4. Divide the highest number in your range by that increment. Divide 8 inches for the axis by this number. Measure this distance from the intersection of the X-axis and Y-axis and draw a mark. Measure the same distance for all marks on the Y-axis. Twenty is the highest number in the sample chart range, and 2 is the increment. Dividing 20 by the increment results in the value of 10. You then divide 8 inches by 10. This gives you 8/10 inch (or 4/5 inch). Measure this distance for the marks on the Y-axis.

5. Next label the marks. Start by labeling the intersection of the X-axis and Y-axis zero. Then label the values of the increments and put these numbers beside the marks above the intersection on the Y-axis. Add the incremental values to the mark values to calculate the number to place at each mark. The Y-axis on Figure 1 begins at zero with increments of 2. Therefore the first mark value is 2. Add the increment value (2) to the mark value 2. Put 4 beside the next mark. Continue adding the increment value to each mark value. Do this until you reach 20.

Plot Values for the X-Axis Items

Use the Y-axis scale to plot values for the X-axis items. Look for the increments on the Y-axis scale that equal the item values on the X scale. If there is not a number equal to that value, place the number on the axis range where it would be approximately equal to that value. Working horizontally, place marks above the items on the X-axis. Repeat this process for all the X-axis items.

In Figure 1, the value for Motor is 5. Since there is no mark with the value 5 on the Y-axis, assume it is between 4 and 6. Place a dot or some other mark at this point directly above Motor on the X-axis.

Draw the Bars

Draw a bar about half the size of the increments between the X-axis marks. The top of the bar is the point plotted and marked for the item as described in Step 3. Draw the bar so your mark is in the middle.

Label the Chart Titles

There are three titles in a chart. The first explains what the chart is about. The second labels the X-axis, describing the items plotted on the axis. The third describes what values are plotted on the Y-axis.

Figure 1 is titled "Customer Complaints in August." The X-axis title is "Type of Complaint" and the Y-axis title is "Number of Complaints."

Applying What You've Learned

This exercise allows the trainees to practice using frequency tables, percentages, and graphs.

Diane works for a pretzel manufacturing company with 2,300 employees. Her quality circle is trying to solve the problem of how to reduce accidents at the plant. Diane was asked to compile data about the type of injuries that have occurred at the plant during the past month. The company nurse provided the following monthly accident report.

Accident Report—Tastee Pretzels, Inc., October

Date	Person	Description of Accident
1	Smith	Tripped over ladder—sprained ankle
3	Rogers	Hand caught in machine—large cut
3	Jackson	Slipped on mopped floor—injured back
5	Cortez	Fell down steps—injured back
6	Gerber	Brushed against ovens—burned hand
8	Mitchell	Tripped over boxes—sprained ankle
9	Walls	Didn't use gloves—burned hand

10	Washington	Fell from ladder—broke leg
12	Ott	Lifted heavy box—injured back
13	Wallace	Solvent splashed—eye injured
13	Michaels	Fell on steps—injured back
15	Chavez	Running and tripped—injured back
16	Jones	Tripped over ladder—sprained ankle
18	DiFabio	Hand caught in machine—large cut
19	Buzan	Slipped on mopped floor—injured back
20	Leveau	Fell down steps—injured back
21	Tillet	Brushed against ovens—burned hand
22	Corte	Tripped over boxes—sprained ankle
23	Davidson	Didn't wear gloves—burned hand
26	Cardamone	Fell from ladder—broke leg
27	Holt	Lifted heavy box—injured back
30	Lilly	Solvent splashed—eye injured
30	Harris	Fell on steps—injured back
31	DeBono	Running and tripped—injured back

■ Create a frequency table for Diane that summarizes the data in the report.

■ Calculate percentages for each item listed in the frequency table. Add another column to the frequency table in Step 1. Write each of the percentages in that column.

■ Draw a bar graph using the frequency table in this exercise.

Creative Thinking

Many people believe they have no creative ability. Often creativity is associated with gifted musicians, artists, or authors. Encourage your students to view creativity in a broader sense. Help them see their creative potential. Finding a solution to any problem is being creative.

Have the group read "Creative Thinking." Encourage them to do the exercises in *Job Savvy*. The solutions to the exercises are at the end of the chapter.

Additional Activity: Toothpick Creations

Divide the class into groups of three. Give each group a box of flat toothpicks. Have them create as many different shapes as possible using the toothpicks.

Additional Activity: Guest Speaker

Ask an inventor or entrepreneur to speak to the class on how they discovered and developed their idea.

Additional Activity: Creative Problem Solving

Have the class brainstorm all types of ways to solve the following problem. Encourage outlandish solutions. Then attempt to make each solution workable.

> Since the new pizza place at the end of the block opened, the Burger Castle where you work has had less business. The manager has asked all employees for ideas to increase business.

Summing Up

Read the "Summing Up" section at the end of the chapter and use the following questions to spark class discussion.

1. Why is problem solving so important to employers?

2. What is meant by *creative thinking*?

3. Why is it important to use all seven steps in the problem-solving process?

Do the Right Thing

Making ethical decisions isn't always easy. Sometimes the ethical answer isn't obvious. The "right" decision can bring conflict with another person. This chapter gives guidelines for making choices when the answers are not clear-cut. Using case studies and class discussions, your students will prepare for real problems they will face in the work world.

A secretary uses the company telephone to make long-distance calls to friends. A mechanic slips a wrench into his lunchbox and takes it home. A marketing representative carries a company secret to a competitor. A salesperson adds a few extra miles to her monthly travel report. Each of these situations deals with ethics.

Ethics are the rules we use to make decisions about life. Our society sets certain ethical rules, and members of society are expected to observe these rules. To ignore those rules in the workplace could result in disciplinary action or even dismissal. In some cases, criminal punishment could result.

Chapter 12 ends with a discussion of several ethical problems common in the workplace. Trainees need to be aware of their responsibility to conduct themselves properly in their job situation. Unethical behavior can result in dismissal; ethical behavior will bring the respect of coworkers and superiors. Most of all, it will increase self-respect.

Activities

Ethical Problems for Business

Read the introduction and the section "Ethical Problems for Business." Discuss the meaning of the word *ethics*. Use the following questions to guide this discussion.

- How are ethical principles formed?

- Why are ethical principles important in a job?

- How could ethical choices affect one's job?

- Why are businesses concerned about ethical behavior?

- What complicates making ethical choices in work situations?

- Who could your ethical decisions affect at work?

To illustrate the difficulty people may have in viewing ethical and unethical behavior, ask the group to respond to the following sentences. "True" or "false" are the only answers allowed.

- Breaking the law is always wrong.

- Speeding is sometimes necessary.

- All drug sales should be illegal.

- The use of alcohol is legal.

- Every citizen should give to charity.

- Accepting charity is a humbling experience.

- Killing is always wrong.

- Wars are sometimes necessary.

Additional Activity: **Journal Assignment**

Have your students write down some ethical values they have and what influenced them in forming these values.

What Is Ethical Behavior?

Have the students read the sections titled "What Is Ethical Behavior?" and "Ethical Decision-Making Problems." Discuss the three basic problems that can cause obstacles in making proper decisions in the workplace. Consider the following questions under each area.

Not knowing what is expected

- Why might you not know how to react in a particular situation?

- How could you handle an unfamiliar situation?

Conflicts in ethical standards

- Who might you conflict with in the workplace?

- How can you behave ethically without causing more conflict?

Dilemmas about a situation

■ Why are some decisions more difficult to make than others?

■ How would you make a decision in an unclear situation?

After reading the case studies, students should write a brief description of how they would handle each situation.

> **Note:** *Don't discuss the situations at this time. This information will be used later in the chapter.*

Guidelines for Making Ethical Decisions

Using this section, discuss each of the questions one might ask to make an ethical decision. Emphasize that before reaching a decision a person should consider more than one of the questions. Listed below are some important issues to stress.

■ **Is it legal?** Each employee is responsible for his or her own behavior. A court of law will not excuse an illegal act resulting from a work order.

■ **How will it make you feel about yourself?** Keeping your self-respect is vital in maintaining your self-esteem.

■ **How do others feel about it?** Seek advice from people you respect. Talking to people with varying viewpoints provides a wider scope of choices. *Be willing to listen to someone who disagrees with you.*

■ **Are you willing to accept responsibility for your decision?** Realize that only you will be held accountable for the action taken.

■ **How would you feel if the whole world knew about it?** If the respect others have for you will be diminished by your behavior, don't do it. *Don't assume that no one will find out.* Even if no one does, you will be afraid someone will.

■ **Does the behavior make sense?** Calmly consider the effects of the behavior.

■ **Will it harm others?** This could include physical, mental, or financial well-being.

- **Will it harm you?** What if you get caught? Is it really worth the risk of punishment?

- **Is the situation fair to everyone involved?** Probably not everyone will benefit from your actions in an equal way, but trying to maintain balance is important. Making a decision that greatly benefits one individual (especially yourself) at the expense of another, is very unwise.

- **Will the people in authority at your organization approve?** Getting information about the situation from authorities (supervisors, managers, employers, the company's lawyer) will allow you to see the organization's viewpoint. *However, authorities are not always ethical.* As an individual, you are responsible for your actions.

- **How would you feel if someone did the same thing to you?** Put yourself in the other person's shoes. How do you want to be treated?

- **Will something bad happen if you don't make a decision?** Perhaps the best approach is to do nothing, but you should consider some questions with this course of action:

  – Do you have all the facts?

  – Is someone else in authority handling the situation?

  – Will the situation resolve itself with time?

Remember, doing nothing when you know someone is being harmed will only cause more problems.

Applying What You've Learned

Divide the class into small groups. Have each group discuss the three case studies. Using the guidelines for making ethical decisions listed earlier, have each group write a solution for each case study, giving reasons for its solutions. In the large-group setting, share the answers and thoughts for the solutions given.

Allow time for students to reevaluate their choices for the five situations presented in "Ethical Decision-Making Problems." The ethical questions should be applied in each situation. Trainees should record any changes they make as well as the reasons for their choices. Now, as a group, go over each of these situations. What was the solution in each case? What ethical questions influenced decisions? Were any students influenced to change their original choices?

Common Ethical Problems

List and discuss the seven ethical problems. Consider the important points under each. As each problem is discussed, add additional ways employees can cheat the company.

- **Favoring friends or relatives.** A company may provide special discounts to employees' families. It's important for employees to know what these benefits are and to whom they apply.

- **Cheating the employer out of time.** In any business, time is money. Using work time for other purposes robs the company.

- **Stealing from the company.** The theft of "small" items is multiplied when many employees are involved. Software piracy can mean dismissal. Discuss freeware, shareware, and copyrights.

- **Abusing drugs and alcohol.** Many companies require drug testing as a part of their employment qualifications.

- **Violating matters of confidentiality.** Employees should know the company's policy on confidentiality.

- **Knowing about other employees' unethical behaviors.** Consider all the consequences if you decide to report another worker's unethical work behavior. Remember, gossip should *never* be the basis for reporting misconduct.

- **Violating the organization's policies.** Knowing the company's policies is important. Breaking these policies could result in disciplinary action.

Note: If you are training for a particular organization, explain the company's policy in each of these areas. What kind of disciplinary action would the company take?

Applying What You've Learned

Divide the class into small groups. Have the group members work together to solve the four case studies. As a large group, discuss each situation and the reasons for each solution.

Summing Up

Read together the chapter summary as a class and use the following questions to spark discussion.

- Why are an employee's ethics important to a company?

- What can result from an employee's unethical behavior?

- Why is it sometimes difficult to make ethical decisions?

Chapter 13

Getting Ahead on the Job

Getting a job is hard work. Keeping that job is work, too. But most workers want even more. They want to advance on their jobs. Often, however, they are confused about what they need to do to get ahead. This chapter explains what employees need to do to get promoted.

My friend Shannon has worked at a daycare center for two years. As a teacher's aide working with young children, Shannon sees no possibility for any type of promotion. The pay rate is low, and no benefits are offered. Discouraged by this job situation, Shannon is ready for a change.

Workers expect to be rewarded for their job performance. In the work world the typical rewards are pay increases and job promotions. Often the new worker has unrealistic ideas of when and how these rewards should come. This chapter presents information on pay raises and promotions. Its approach is general, since company policies vary so much.

Learning to set realistic career goals early can help new workers progress. If they spend some time thinking about these goals, they can approach their careers in a much more organized way.

Few people remain in the same job their entire work experience. Knowing how and why to leave a job is important not only to trainees but to experienced workers as well. The final section of Chapter 13 discusses reasons for leaving a job and how to tell the company you are quitting.

Activities

You, Incorporated

Have trainees read the chapter introduction. Ask the following questions:

- How many of you want to take home the pay you get now for the rest of your life?

- How many of you want to stay in the same position in your company for the rest of your life?

Now have the class brainstorm a list of ways an employer lets workers know they are doing a good job. (Pay raises and promotions will probably be among the suggestions.)

Have the students read the section titled "You, Incorporated.". Compile a list of skills your trainees have. Write the list on a flip chart or overhead. Discuss what skills they can improve or new skills they can learn.

Getting a Raise

Discuss the six common instances when employers give pay raises. Be sure the trainees understand that not every company follows these policies. They should ask their supervisor about their company's pay raise policy.

> **Note:** *If you are training for a particular organization, this is a good time to present the company's policies on pay raises.*

Additional Activity: To Raise or Not to Raise?
Use the questions below to guide group discussion.

- Why might a raise be given after a worker completes probation?

- How long can the probation period last?

- How do incentive increases determine a worker's raise?

- How often might a worker be evaluated using incentive increases?

- Why might the ability to get along with others be important in receiving an incentive increase?

- What is the meaning of *inflation*?

- What does a cost-of-living increase do for a worker?

- Why might an employer offer a raise in an attempt to keep an employee?

- What is the risk to employees of telling their employer they can get more money in a different job?

- What are some added job responsibilities that could result in a pay raise?

■ What are some new skills an employee might acquire that could result in a pay raise?

■ Why does a pay raise often accompany a promotion?

The Difference Between Wage and Salary

Discuss the information in the box, "The Difference Between Wage and Salary." Emphasize that salaried workers often have more responsibilities.

Be sure the group understands that salaried workers do not receive overtime pay, although they may be required to work more than an eight-hour day. Many entry-level employees do not realize this.

Applying What You've Learned

Divide the class into four groups. Assign one of the four case studies to each group. Using the questions as guidelines, ask the groups to discuss their case studies. Have each group share their opinions with the entire class.

Additional Activity: Role-Play

Divide the class into new groups and assign one of the case studies to each. Each group should write out a role-play between the person and supervisor in the case study. In each case, the person should ask for a pay raise and give the reasons for the raise. Members of each group can present their role-play to the entire class.

Getting Promoted

Allow time for each individual to read this section. What are the two major criteria for promotions? Be sure the group understands the meaning of each term. Use the following questions to spark group discussion:

■ If a pay raise is given with a promotion, what might a worker assume about the new position?

■ Why might a salaried worker in a promotion position not get as large a raise as expected?

■ Why does a promotion increase a person's status?

■ How does a promotion result in a greater challenge to a worker?

■ Why does a promotion increase one's self-esteem?

Now use the following questions to spark a discussion on how to get promoted:

■ Who knows about job openings within your organization?

■ Who might be included in your network?

■ What is meant by the term *posting*?

■ What can a worker do to develop a good reputation?

■ What is meant by the term *networking*?

■ How can a worker "create his or her own job?"

> **Note:** *If you are training for a particular organization, this is a good time to present the company's policies on promotions.*

Additional Activity: Promotability

Brainstorm a list of items that could influence a supervisor to promote an employee. Write the list of ideas on a flip chart or overhead.

Additional Activity: Journal Assignment

Have the students write a paragraph to complete the following statement:

■ I should be promoted to the position of because I ...

When Promotions Occur

Allow time for individuals to read and complete this section. Have the group make a list of all the skills a worker needs to get a promotion. Post this list. Use the list to do the case studies in "Applying What You've Learned."

Applying What You've Learned

Divide the class into small groups. Have the groups answer the case study questions using the posted list of skills to make their decisions. Then have the groups share their choices and the reasons in each case. There may be some disagreement among the groups, but there need not be a consensus. Use this opportunity to illustrate that making a decision about promoting someone is not always easy

Career Development

Discuss the meaning of the term *career development*. Together go through the topics listed in this section.

Additional Activity: CEI

The Career Exploration Inventory (CEI), is designed for exploration of work, leisure activities, and education or learning. Use this simple, self-scoring device to help your trainees identify career areas of interest. (The *CEI* is available from JIST Works.)

Additional Activity: Progress Report

Divide the class into groups of three. Each group should choose an entry-level job. Using the questions in the bulleted list, have each group write a career progression plan.

Additional Activity: Journal Assignment

Ask the students to write down a career plan for themselves.

Additional Activity: Video Presentation

Show the video *Job Survival Skills: It's a Jungle Out There!* (available from JIST Works). This 18-minute video has two parts: "How to Avoid Getting Fired" and "How to Get Ahead on the Job."

Leaving a Job

Have the class read this section. Discuss the reasons for leaving a job. Discuss the suggestions for preparing to leave a job.

Divide the class into small groups. Have each group answer the following questions:

- What are some reasons for leaving a job?

- How soon should you tell your employer you are leaving?

- If you aren't sure how to resign, who could advise you?

- Why should you have another job waiting before you resign from your present job?

- Imagine you are leaving your job because your supervisor is treating you unfairly. How do you tell your supervisor you're leaving?

- What are some things you may be required to do before you leave the job?

- Why is it important to leave a job with good relationships if at all possible?

Applying What You've Learned

Divide the class into groups of three. Have the groups read and discuss the two case studies and come to a group decision about each case. Ask each group to share its answers.

Summing Up

Read the summary of the chapter and use the following questions for class discussion:

- What are some things a worker can do to earn promotions and pay raises?

- What is the difference between wage and salary?

- How can planning help in your career development?

- What are some important things to remember about leaving a job?

On-the-Job Training Guide

Job Savvy can be used to train workers either in the classroom or in one-on-one situations. This section of the *Instructor's Guide* provides information employers can use to train new employees. You may find that another approach is more effective for your organization, but the information here will help you get started.

Much of the material in this book could be covered in a two-day orientation session or during the first two weeks of employment. It is designed to be used by supervisors as they instruct new workers starting on the job.

Student Preparation for Lesson 1

Have new employees read the first three chapters of *Job Savvy* before coming to their first day of work. Tell them there will be a short quiz on each chapter.

Lesson 1

1. Give the employees a quiz on Chapters 1 through 3. Use five questions from the Question Bank for each chapter. Go over the results and discuss questions the employees answered incorrectly. If any of your trainees have answered more than one-third of the questions incorrectly, it's doubtful they actually read the material. At the very least, they don't understand it. Attempt to find out what the problem is and try to correct it.

2. Ask the employees what they found most interesting about Chapter 1.

3. Use information from Chapter 1 to discuss the following points.

   ▓ How your company is affected by labor market trends

   ▓ The diversity of the workforce in your business and the behavior expected from workers interacting with people from different ethnic backgrounds

   ▓ The ways your company uses permanent, temporary, and contract workers

4. Ask the employees to describe personal skills that make them desirable employees. Refer them to Chapter 2 to identify the skills employers value most.

5. Use this opportunity to describe what you expect from new employees.

6. Talk to the employees about their new jobs. Chapter 3 provides a thorough checklist for orientation sessions.

7. You may want to give the employees two hours to read and complete the exercises in Chapters 4 and 5. If you don't have time for this, you can cover the material verbally and ask the employees to read those chapters later.

8. Review Chapter 4 and talk about dress codes for your business.

9. Review Chapter 5. Ask the employees to talk about how they plan to get to work on time every day they are scheduled to work. Describe what your business expects of employees in regard to attendance and punctuality.

10. You may want to give the employees an hour to read and complete the exercises in Chapter 6.

11. Discuss the information in Chapter 6. Describe the resources your business makes available to help employees learn about their jobs. Take this time to do the following:

    ■ Go over each employee's job description and review each major task that is part of that job.

    ■ Train the employees on those tasks that must be mastered immediately. Remember to use the following time-proven method for on-the-job training.

        – Tell each trainee how to do the task.

        – Demonstrate how to do the task. Explain each step as you go through the process.

        – Have the trainee do the task. Carefully watch each step and provide feedback.

        – Have the trainee practice the task several times. Continue this process until you are sure the trainee can perform the task adequately.

12. Show the video *You've Got the Job ... Now What?* This is a good summary of the information covered in this lesson. It will reinforce the information you've covered with the employees so far.

Student Preparation for Lesson 2

Have the trainees read Chapters 7 and 8. Explain that a quiz will be given at your next meeting.

Lesson 2

1. Provide a quiz on Chapters 7 and 8. Use five questions from the Question Bank for each chapter. Discuss the questions that were answered incorrectly.

2. Ask the trainees to describe their top three self-management skills, transferable skills, and specific job skills. Provide feedback about how each of these skills can contribute to success at work.

3. Ask the employees to describe the most interesting points of Chapter 8. Explain your job. Describe the expectations your manager has for your performance. Identify five things the employees can do to get along with you most effectively. This is a time to expand on the expectations discussed in the first lesson.

4. You may want to give the employees an hour to read Chapter 9.

5. Review the major points in Chapter 9. What's important for the employees to know about getting along with others in their assigned work areas? Ask them to explain the concept of teamwork. How accurate is this concept as it relates to your company?

6. Take this opportunity to introduce the trainees to other employees if you haven't already done so. You might want to arrange a short meeting with other employees to have them describe the following:

   - What do they expect from new workers?

   - What should new workers do when they need assistance from coworkers?

   - What tips do they have for new employees?

   - What is the one thing they would most like to tell new employees?

   - You should allow the new employees an opportunity to ask a few questions.

7. You may want to give the employees an hour to read Chapter 10.

8. Discuss the type of contact the trainees will have with customers. Explain the company's policies on customer service. Have the trainees observe

other workers as they interact with customers. Have them answer these questions:

- What did coworkers do that appeared to provide good customer service?

- In what ways did they provide poor customer service?

Also have them write down questions they have about customer service.

9. This is a good opportunity to explain how to use the telephone system. After demonstrating how the system works, discuss customer contacts on the phone. Tell the trainees how the phone is to be answered. Describe how they are to take messages and get them to the proper individuals.

10. Have the employees watch the video *Working 9 to 5*, which summarizes many of the points covered in this lesson.

Student Preparation for Lesson 3

Have the employees read Chapters 11 to 13. Inform them that there will be a quiz on these chapters.

Lesson 3

1. Give a quiz over Chapters 11 through 13. Use five questions from the Question Bank for each chapter. Discuss any questions that were answered incorrectly.

2. Explain how your company uses some of the problem-solving techniques described in Chapter 11. Describe some problems your organization has solved recently.

3. Identify a common but easily solved problem in the organization and have the employees use problem-solving techniques to find possible solutions. Discuss the solutions and explain the strengths and weaknesses of each.

4. Use the case studies in Chapter 12 to identify ethical problems that are common at your company. Have the employees respond to these case studies.

5. Chapter 12 discusses ethical issues related to the computer. Discuss proper employee behavior in regard to e-mail, use of the Internet, copying software, and information stored on computers.

6. Chapter 13 allows you to discuss several important points, including these:

   ▪ Policies and procedures for awarding raises

   ▪ Policies and procedures for getting promoted

   ▪ Opportunities to advance on the job

   ▪ Job opportunities other employees have moved into

   ▪ Common job openings that occur in the company

   ▪ Skills the employees should work on to move up in the company

   ▪ Individuals who might be willing to act as mentors

   ▪ Opportunities for training and how to take advantage of these

7. Show the video *Career Tips for Your Future*, which summarizes many of the points covered in this lesson.

Conclusion

Congratulate the employees for completing training designed to help them be successful on the job. Remind them of the skills they identified and how these can contribute to their success at work. Finally, give them several specific objectives to accomplish in the first two weeks on the job.

Introduction to the Video Series

How to Be a Success at Work

An award-winning series of three videos based on *Job Savvy* is available from JIST Works. These videos provide an excellent supplement to the book. You can use them in a variety of ways:

1. **Show them to a class as an introduction to the material covered in the book.** Each video presents a summary of the information presented in the book and can be used to present the topics that will be covered in class.

2. **Use them to summarize the material covered.** After you've presented the material in a range of chapters, show the video. Then ask the class to identify the most important points they have learned.

3. **Present the section of each video that corresponds to a chapter being studied.** The material below gives both an outline and the location of the subject matter on the video. This helps you locate the portion of the video you can use for each subject.

4. **Use them for on-the-job training.**

Instructors find that students pay more attention to videos in class when they know there will be a quiz about the video. At the end of this appendix you'll find a quiz on the video material.

Answers to Video Quiz You've Got the Job . . . Now What?

1. T   2. F   3. T   4. F   5. F   6. T   7. T   8. T   9. F   10. T

Answers to Video Quiz Working 9 to 5

1. F   2. T   3. F   4. T   5. T   6. F   7. F   8. T   9. F   10. T

Answers to Video Quiz Career Tips for Your Future

1. F   2. F   3. T   4. T   5. F   6. T   7. T   8. F   9. T   10. F

You've Got the Job ... Now What?

- ▇ **Total run time:** Approximately 13 minutes

- ▇ *Job Savvy* **material covered:** Chapters 1 through 6

- ▇ **Purpose:** Viewers will develop an understanding of the basic expectations of the employer as they start a new job and learn how to get off to a good start.

- ▇ **Objectives:** Viewers will learn to:

1. Explain the importance of attendance

2. State specific ways to improve attendance and punctuality

3. Describe grooming and dress appropriate for the workplace

4. Identify how to have a successful first day on the job

5. Explain the importance of learning to adapt and grow in the workplace

Outline

1. **Getting to work on time** (approximate time: 2:15)

2. **Dress, hygiene, and good grooming habits** (approximate time: 3:40)

3. **The first day at a new job** (approximate time: 5:25)

4. **Getting off to a good start on a new job** (approximate time: 7:10)

5. **Attendance and punctuality** (approximate time: 8:25)

6. **Employer expectations** (approximate time: 10:40)

7. **Learning on the job** (approximate time: 12:25)

Working 9 to 5

- **Total run time:** Approximately 13 minutes

- *Job Savvy* **material covered:** Chapters 7 through 10

- **Purpose:** Viewers will discover the importance of relationships on the job and how to build positive relationships.

- **Objectives:** Viewers will learn to:

1. Improve their self-image

2. Identify their skills

3. Develop a successful relationship with their supervisor

4. Become effective team members

Outline

1. **Understanding and believing in yourself** (approximate time: 2:10)

2. **Skills you need for success** (approximate time: 5:15)

3. **Getting along with the supervisor** (approximate time: 7:45)

4. **Getting along with coworkers** (approximate time: 10:45)

Career Tips for Your Future

- **Total run time:** Approximately 14 minutes

- *Job Savvy* **material covered:** Chapters 11 through 13

- **Purpose:** Viewers will learn to achieve a higher level of performance at work.

- **Objectives:** Learners will learn to:

1. Implement the problem-solving process

2. Make ethical decisions

3. Describe how raises and promotions are given in most organizations

Outline

1. **Problem-solving skills** (approximate time: 1:45)

2. **Ethical behavior in the workplace** (approximate time 6:10)

3. **Getting pay raises and promotions** (approximate time: 11:50)

You've Got the Job . . . Now What?
Video Quiz

Read the following statements. Put a "T" beside each true statement and an "F" beside each false one.

_____ 1.   It is possible to plan for special conditions that might make you late for a job.

_____ 2.   You shouldn't worry about calling your supervisor when you are going to be absent from work. He or she will figure out that you aren't coming in.

_____ 3.   You should shower or bathe every day.

_____ 4.   You should follow your own personal taste when dressing for work.

_____ 5.   You can complete payroll deduction forms without any special information.

_____ 6.   Your lifestyle affects your ability to have good attendance at work.

_____ 7.   Adjusting to a new job is easier when you find another worker who is willing to be a "buddy."

_____ 8.   Drinking alcoholic beverages on the job can get you fired.

_____ 9.   Organizations need workers who don't want to change because they add stability to the business.

_____10.   You should take advantage of all learning opportunities your employer offers.

Working 9 to 5
Video Quiz

Read the following statements. Put a "T" beside each true statement and an "F" beside each false one.

_____ 1. A person's self-image is improved when he or she believes that success is based on fate.

_____ 2. Joe Girard suggests that you "pat yourself on the back" at least once a day.

_____ 3. Job-related skills are those you need for managing your personal life at work.

_____ 4. Transferable skills are those that can be used in a variety of jobs.

_____ 5. Following instructions is an example of a self-management skill.

_____ 6. Most businesses emphasize individual achievement over team work.

_____ 7. Supervisors are important to your career because they tell you what you should do.

_____ 8. You should discuss your job performance with your supervisor.

_____ 9. When coworkers tease you, you should let them know right away that you don't appreciate it.

_____10. You must learn to work with a diversity of people.

Career Tips for Your Future *Video Quiz*

Read the following statements. Put a "T" beside each true statement and an "F" beside each false one.

_____ 1. Problem-solving skills are important for supervisors but not for front-line workers.

_____ 2. Brainstorming is an important technique for analyzing the cause of a problem.

_____ 3. The final step in the problem-solving process is evaluating the results.

_____ 4. Most people develop their basic ethical beliefs when they are young.

_____ 5. The only important principle for making an ethical decision is to ask if it's legal.

_____ 6. One good way to decide if something is ethical is to ask yourself if you would want someone to do the same thing to you.

_____ 7. A common ethical problem is cheating the employer by wasting time talking.

_____ 8. You should always tell your employer when you know something negative about a coworker.

_____ 9. One reason an employer may give a raise is to keep a worker from leaving.

_____ 10. The only reason for working is to gain material things.

Appendix C

Overhead Master Transparencies for Chapters 1-13

Labor Force Trends

Slower Growth Expected
12% growth from 1995 to 2005
16% growth from 1982 to 1993

More Participation by Women
46% of labor force in 1997
48% by 2005

Labor Force Aging
Baby boomers will be 45-64 years old in 2005

More Ethnic Diversity
Ethnic composition by year 2005:
Blacks: 12%
Hispanic Origin: 7.5%
Asian: 2.6%
Native Americans: 0.8%

Organizations and Work, 1994

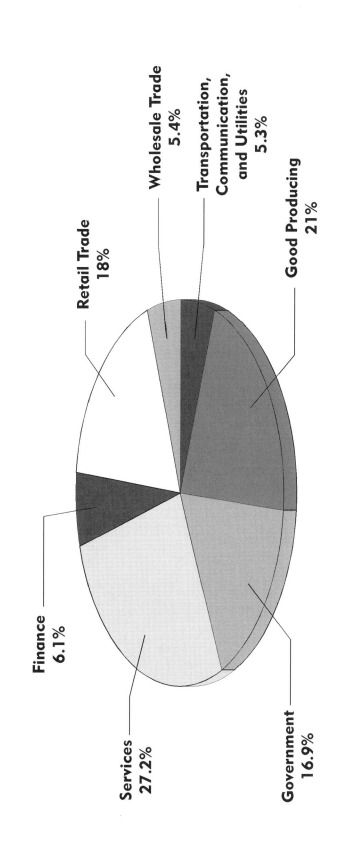

Wholesale Trade
5.4%

Transportation,
Communication,
and Utilities
5.3%

Good Producing
21%

Retail Trade
18%

Finance
6.1%

Services
27.2%

Government
16.9%

Organizations and Work, 2005

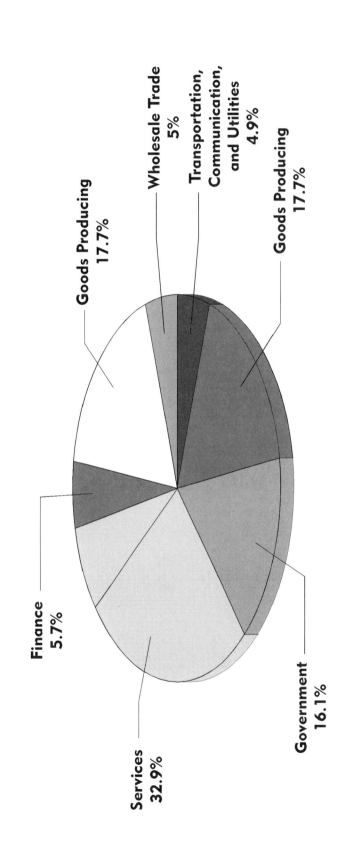

Wholesale Trade
5%

Transportation,
Communication,
and Utilities
4.9%

Goods Producing
17.7%

Goods Producing
17.7%

Finance
5.7%

Government
16.1%

Services
32.9%

Chapter 1 - Transparency 3

Education and Earnings

Level of Education	Avg. Monthly Earnings	Difference
No High School Diploma	$ 508	N/A
High School Diploma	$1,080	0
Vocational Certificate	$1,303	21%
Some College – no degree	$1,375	27%
College Degree	$2,339	117%
Advanced Degree	$3,331	208%
Professional Degree	$5,067	369%

Chapter 1 - Transparency 4

173

Structure of Work

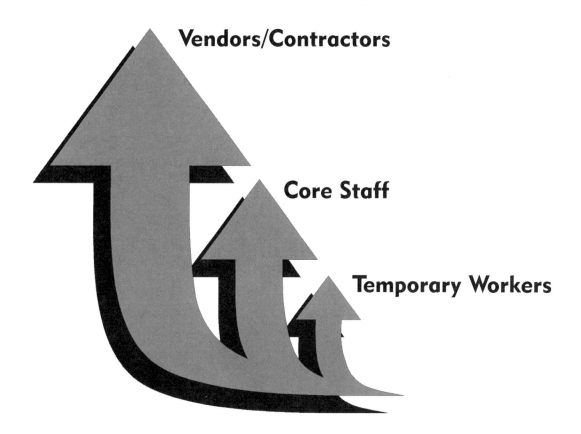

Vendors/Contractors

Core Staff

Temporary Workers

Organization of the New Workplace

SCANS Skills

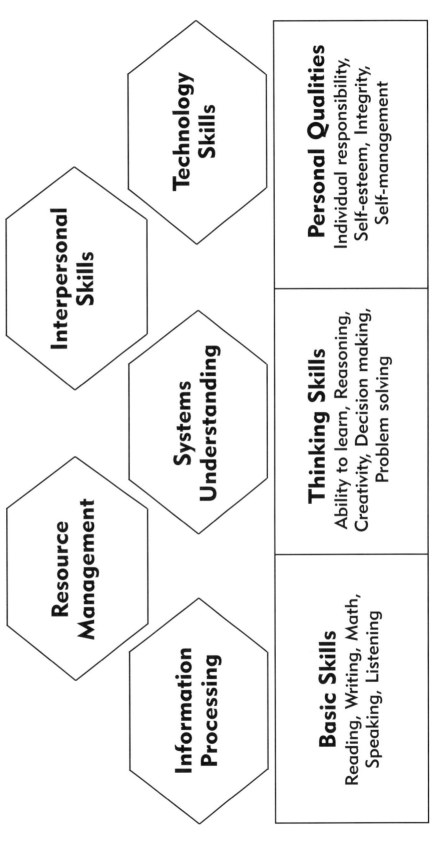

Resource Management

Interpersonal Skills

Systems Understanding

Technology Skills

Information Processing

Basic Skills
Reading, Writing, Math, Speaking, Listening

Thinking Skills
Ability to learn, Reasoning, Creativity, Decision making, Problem solving

Personal Qualities
Individual responsibility, Self-esteem, Integrity, Self-management

ASTD Workplace Basics Study

Seven Basic Skills Employers Want

1. Knowing how to learn

2. Reading, writing, and computation

3. Listening and oral communication

4. Adaptability

5. Personal management

6. Group effectiveness

7. Influence

Study conducted by the American Society for Training and Development (ASTD)

Dependability vs. Reliability

Dependability: You will be on time and at work every day. You will notify your supervisor when you cannot be at work.

Reliability: You will follow through with a job. You look for things to do after completing assigned tasks.

Business Basics

High Quality

Customer Satisfaction

Your Company

Profitability

10 Self-Management Skills Employers Want in Employees

1. Concern for productivity

2. Pride of craftsmanship and quality of work

3. Responsibility

4. Reliability

5. Work habits

6. Attitudes toward company and employer

7. Ability to write and speak effectively

8. Ability to read and apply printed matter

9. Ability to follow instructions

10. Ambition/motivation/desire to get ahead

Reasons Workers Like Their Jobs

Reason I like work	Positive responses
Open communication	65%
Effects on family/personal life	60%
Nature of work	59%
Management quality	59%
Supervisor	58%
Control over work	55%
Gain new skills	55%
Job security	54%
Coworker quality	53%
Job location	50%
Stimulating work	50%

What's Important to Workers

What's important	Rank
Job security	1
Compensation	2
Benefit costs	3
Job satisfaction	4
Career advancement	5
Recognition	6
Dependent care	7
Work environment	8
Job training	9
Vacation time	10

What to Expect on the First Day of Work

1. Reporting to work
Dress appropriately
Know where to go and who to contact
Bring required documentation

2. Orientation
Introduction
Payroll and personnel information
Policies and practices review
Benefits/services review
Employer expectations

3. Introduction to the job
Work instructions
Supplies and equipment
Telephone system
Breaks

4. Introduction and tour
Key people
Supplies
Equipment

Chapter 3 - Transparency 1

Typical Benefits Provided by Business

Type of Benefit	Small Business	Large Business
Paid vacations	88%	92%
Paid holidays	82%	96%
Paid sick leave	53%	67%
Medical care	71%	83%
Dental care	33%	60%
Life insurace	64%	94%
Retirement plan	45%	59%

Chapter 3 - Transparency 2

Tips for Adjusting to the New Job

1. Be positive

2. Ask for help

3. Don't be a know-it-all

4. Have a good sense of humor

5. Find a buddy

6. Follow instructions

7. Read company policies

8. Determine evaluation policies

Percentage of Businesses with Casual Dress Codes

Type of Policy	1995	1992
Casual every day	33%	20%
Casual one day per week	42%	17%
No casual days	10%	37%
Occasional casual days	15%	27%

Guidelines for Dress at Work

1. **Follow dress codes**

2. **Dress appropriately for the workplace**

3. **Make sure clothes are neat and clean**

4. **Follow requirements for uniforms**

5. **Wear required safety clothing**

Grooming Habits for the Workplace

1. Shower or bathe daily

2. Use deodorant

3. Brush teeth

4. Gargle with mouthwash

5. Shave

6. Shampoo hair

7. Trim or style hair

8. Trim fingernails

9. Use makeup appropriately

Problems Caused by Absenteeism and Tardiness

1. Problems for the employer
Reduced productivity
Customer dissatisfaction

2. Problems for supervisors
Rearrange work schedules
More work for supervisor

3. Problems for coworkers
Scheduling problems
Additional work

4. Problems for the employee
Lost pay
Hostility from supervisor and coworkers

Healthy Lifestyles = Success on the job

- Get a good night's sleep

- Eat well

- Exercise regularly

- Avoid smoking

- Avoid excessive alcohol consumption

- Avoid drugs

- Keep good company

- Socialize with coworkers

Five Steps to Ensure Good Work Attendance

1. Have reliable transportation

2. Use reliable child care

3. Use a calendar

4. Plan a schedule with your supervisor

5. Call the employer

Planning Calendar

Sun	Mon	Tues	Wed	Thurs	Fri	Sat

Getting to Work on Time

You need to. . .

1. Get a reliable alarm clock

2. Get up early

3. Plan for special conditions

4. Notify your supervisor if you are delayed

Improve Your Learning

- Assume responsibility for and control for learning

- Apply what you learn—quickly

- Use experience to improve learning

- Understand why learning is important

- Take time to learn and practice

- Be comfortable with your learning pace

- Use association

- Use the whole-part-whole approach

Chapter 6 - Transparency 1

Education for Life

"There is no one education,
no one skill, that lasts a
lifetime now."

—Futurist John Naisbitt

Know Your Learning Style

- Reading
- Listening
- Observing
- Talking

- Doing
- Participating
- Smelling/Tasting

Steps to Learning

Step 1   Motivate yourself

Step 2   Set objectives

Step 3   Identify resources

Step 4   Choose the best resources

Step 5   Schedule the project

Step 6   Write down questions

Step 7   Complete the project

Step 8   Evaluate progress

Step 9   Practice

Chapter 6 - Transparency 4

© 1998, JIST Works, Inc., Indianapolis, Indiana

Building a Healthy Self-Concept

- Tell yourself you are number one every morning.

- Write "I believe in myself" on cards, and place them where you will see them frequently.

- Associate with other winners—avoid losers.

- Do away with negative thoughts.

- Pat yourself on the back at lease once a day.

- Repeat "I will" at least 10 times each day.

- Do the things you fear the most to prove to yourself you can successfully accomplish them.

—Based on information from Joe Girard.

Chapter 7 - Transparency 1

Know Your Skills

1. Self-Management Skills

Punctual   Honest
Reliable   Patient
Follow instructions   Self-motivated

2. Transferable Skills

Speaking in public   Planning
Supervising others   Increasing sales
Problem solving   Instructing others

3. Job-Related/Result of Training Skills

Computer skills
Medical-related skills
Operating a forklift

223

Believe in Yourself

- **Think positive**
- **Accept compliments**
- **Accept responsiblity**
- **Identify your skills**
- **Reward yourself**

Supervision:
"In short, it is getting people to make what we have into what we want."

—Thomas Von der Embse

Principles of Good "Followership"

- **Don't blame the boss**

- **Don't fight the boss**

- **Use initiative**

- **Accept responsibility**

- **Tell the truth and don't quibble**

- **Do your homework**

- **Be willing to implement suggestions you make**

- **Keep the boss informed**

- **Fix problems when they occur**

- **Put in an honest day's work**

—U.S. Air Force Colonel Phillip Meilinger

Chapter 8 - Transparency 2

Communicating with Your Supervisor

Remember . . .

1. You must be able to follow instructions.

2. You need to know how to ask questions.

3. You should report any problems and results of your work.

4. You need to accurately record and forward messages.

5. You need to discuss your job performance.

Chapter 8 - Transparency 3

© *1998, JIST Works, Inc., Indianapolis, Indiana*

Learn to Follow Instructions

- Concentrate
- Listen
- Watch
- Question
- Write
- Practice

Communicating About Job Performance

Don't respond to feedback with anger

Know what it is you have done wrong

Thank your supervisor for compliments

Ask for feedback

Meeting Your Supervisor's Expectations

■ **Be truthful**

■ **Don't extend your breaks**

■ **Get your work done**

■ **Be cooperative**

■ **Be adaptive**

■ **Take the initiative**

Conflict Resolution

Resolving Problems with Your Supervisor:

1. Don't accuse

2. State your feelings

3. Ask for feedback

4. State what you want

5. Get a commitment

6. Compromise when necessary

Be a Team Player

Know your position

Accept good-natured teasing

Do your fair share

Don't do other people's work

Know how your team functions

Values are the importance we give to ideas, things, or people.

Three General Categories:

1. Traditionalist

Hard work, loyalty to the organization, authority of leaders

2. Humanist

Quality of life, autonomy, loyalty to self, leaders attentive to worker's needs

3. Pragmatist

Success, achievement, loyalty to career, reward people for hard work

Temperaments

1. Optimists . . .

are impulsive
enjoy the immediate
enjoy action for action's sake
like working with things

2. Realists . . .

like to belong to groups
feel obligations strongly
have a strong work ethic
need order

3. Futurists . . .

like to control things
want to be highly competent
are the most self-critical
strive for excellence

4. Idealists . . .

are in search of their "self"
want to know the meaning of things
appreciate people

Chapter 9 - Transparency 3

Basic Human Relations

- Get to know other workers

- Don't try to change everything

- Be honest

- Be direct

- Avoid gossip

- Be positive and supportive

- Show appreciation

- Share credit when it's deserved

- Return favors

- Live in the present

- Ask for help and/or advice

- Avoid "battles"

- Follow group standards

- Take interest in your coworkers' jobs

Good Electronic Manners

Leave short, concise voice mail messages

Give essential information in voice mail messages

Keep voice mail greetings short

Don't leave angry voice mail messages

Don't read another person's fax messages

Call before sending a fax

Follow company e-mail policies

Avoid negative communications through e-mail

Be cautious about copying e-mail messages to inappropriate people

Avoid "flaring" when communicating by e-mail

Respect the privacy of other workers' computers and disks

Workplace Harassment Examples

Sexual Harassment

Unwanted stares

Touching another person

Telling sexual jokes

Commenting on sexual characteristics

Displaying nude pictures/obscene cartoons

Racial Harassment

Telling racist jokes

Using racist slurs

Commenting on racial characterstics

Distributing racist materials

Excluding someone from company activities because of race

Reasons Businesses Lose Customers

Reason for not returning	Percentage
Died	1%
Moved away	3%
Influenced by friends	5%
Lured away by competition	9%
Dissatisfied with product	14%
Indifferent employee	68%

Basics of Good Customer Service

- Have a positive attitude

- Make the customer feel good

- Pleasantly and immediately greet customers

- Exceed the customer's expectations

Listening to Customers

- **Be attentive**

- **Listen without interruption**

- **Ask questions to clarify needs**

- **Repeat what you understand the customer's need to be**

- **Negotiate the final result**

Basic Customer Needs

- **Friendliness**

- **Understanding and empathy**

- **Fairness**

- **Control**

- **Options and alternatives**

- **Information**

Customer Service Tips for the Telephone

- **Promptly answer the phone**

- **Use an appropriate greeting**

- **Listen to customers**

- **Take action when possible**

- **Put the customer on hold *after* getting permission**

- **Transfer customer call, letting customer know what is being done**

- **Take a message when necessary**

The Problem-Solving Process

1. Identify the problem

2. Gather and organize data about the problem

3. Develop solutions to the problem

4. Evaluate possible solutions

5. Select the best solution

6. Implement the solution

7. Evaluate the solution

Developing Solutions

- **Talk to other people**

- **Hold a group discussion**
  Brainstorm
  Nominal Group Technique

- **Change places with other employees**

- **Visit other organizations with similar problem**

- **Read about the problem**

Nine Dot Problem-Solving Exercise

Data Collection Frequency Table

Problem	Tally		Percentage
Motor quits working	ⵒⵒ	5	10%
Handle breaks	ⵒⵒ ⵒⵒ ⵒⵒⵒ	14	28%
Starter won't work	‖	3	6%
Oil leaks	ⵒⵒ ⵒⵒ ⵒ	11	22%
Blade falls off	ⵒⵒ ‖	7	14%
Tires fall off	‖‖	4	8%
Controls won't work	ⵒⵒ ⵒ	6	12%

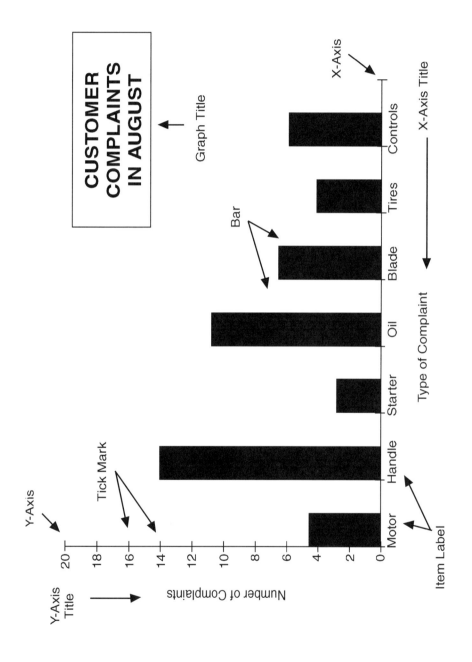

CUSTOMER COMPLAINTS IN AUGUST

Graph Title

X-Axis

X-Axis Title

Bar

Y-Axis

Tick Mark

Y-Axis Title

Number of Complaints

Type of Complaint

Item Label

Motor · Handle · Starter · Oil · Blade · Tires · Controls

Ethics

are principles or standards that govern our behavior and actions.

Guidelines for Making Ethical Decisions

1. Is it legal?

2. How will it make you feel about yourself?

3. How do others feel about it?

4. How would you feel if the whole world knew about it?

5. Does the behavior make sense?

6. Is the situation fair to everyone?

7. Will people in authority approve?

8. How would you feel if someone did the same thing to you?

9. Will something bad happen if you don't make a decision?

Common Ethical Problems in the Workplace

- **Favoring** friends or relatives

- **Cheating** the employer out of time

- **Stealing** from the company

- **Abusing** drugs and alcohol

- **Violating** matters of confidentiality

- **Knowing** about other employees' unethical behaviors

- **Violating** company policies

You, Incorporated

Skills are what you have to sell to an employer

Improve your skills through education and experience

Market your skills

Stretch out and learn new skills that you can sell

Getting a Raise

When employers give raises . . .

- Upon completion of probation

- As incentive increases

- As cost-of-living increases

- To keep employees

- To reward special efforts

- For new assignments

On the Road to a Promotion

Tips:

1. Keep track of job openings

2. Talk to your supervisor

3. Notify the Human Resources Department

4. Create a network

5. Develop a good reputation

6. Create your own job

Career Development

Reaching your personal goals in work and in life . . .

1. Explore job possibilities

2. Identify your skills and abilities

3. Know your values

4. Set a goal

5. Develop a career path

6. Write your plan

7. Find a mentor

8. Keep a record of your accomplishments

9. Review your plan

10. Change your plans when necessary

Don't Burn Your Bridges

When leaving a job . . .

1. Have another job waiting

2. Give reasonable notice

3. Be tactful

4. Know the expectations

5. Don't be disruptive

Question Bank

What follows are quiz questions
for each chapter of Job Savvy
including fill-in-the-blank,
true-or-false, and multiple-choice.
(Sometimes one question
has been written in two
or more styles.)

Chapter 1 Test Questions

Part 1. Fill in the Blank

Fill in the missing word or words in each sentence.

1. People who are available and want to work make up the _____ in this country.

2. The laborforce of the future will be more diversified in gender, age, and _____ groups.

3. The growing number of women in the workforce has caused many businesses to become _____ workplaces.

4. Some businesses recruit 14- and 15-year-olds for _____ wage jobs.

5. _____ has a great effect on how much a person earns.

6. Many businesses use _____ employment services to provide a flexible laborforce.

7. _____ workers are hired and work full-time as permanent employees.

8. Having an education will help you get a job, keep a job, and earn _____ in your lifetime.

9. _____ training programs help workers learn to appreciate other workers' cultural backgrounds.

10. "Fast food" is only one business in the _____ producing economy in this country.

Part 2. Multiple Choice

Circle the letter that best completes each statement.

1. The increase of women in the workforce has made business more aware of issues such as:

   a. child care.

   b. job sharing.

   c. flex-time.

   d. family leave.

   e. all of the above

2. "Family-friendly" business practices are being demanded by

    a. women working in service industries.

    b. ethnic groups.

    c. both men and women.

    d. younger workers in minimum-wage jobs.

    e. self-employed workers.

3. Workers in service-producing businesses include

    a. real estate agents.

    b. coal miners.

    c. factory workers.

    d. carpenters.

    e. none of the above

4. The laborforce

    a. has no effect on business.

    b. is composed mostly of white males.

    c. is made up of adults ages 18 to 65 in this country.

    d. is getting older.

    e. all of the above

5. The fastest-growing percentage of jobs in the labor market are

    a. low-paying jobs.

    b. jobs requiring more education.

    c. jobs requiring little education.

    d. jobs having higher pay.

    e. all of the above

6. As the workforce ages businesses may

    a. avoid hiring older workers.

    b. lay off older workers.

    c. explore ways to use workers regardless of age.

    d. ask workers to retire sooner.

    e. none of the above

7. Contingent workers

    a. receive many fringe benefits from employers.

    b. make up about 25 percent of the workforce.

    c. have permanent jobs.

    d. have job security.

    e. are not used by most businesses.

8. Over half of the laborforce is working

    a. for companies that produce goods.

    b. as temporary workers.

    c. for small businesses that employ 250 or fewer workers.

    d. part-time

    e. for the government.

9. Businesses use subcontractors

    a. to work on specific projects.

    b. to work underground.

    c. as core employees.

    d. as long-term employees.

    e. none of the above

10. The workforce is expected

    a. to include fewer women until the year 2005.

    b. to grow smaller through the year 2005.

    c. to show a decrease of workers from ethnic groups.

    d. to decrease as the Baby Boom generation ages.

    e. to show no effect as the Baby Boom generation ages.

Part 3. True or False

Read the following statements. Put a "T" beside each true statement and an "F" beside each false one.

_____ 1. The future workforce will include more differences in gender, age, and ethnic background.

_____ 2. The lifetime earnings of a college graduate will be greater than those of a high school graduate.

_____ 3. Hospitals, government agencies, and retail stores are goods-producing organizations.

_____ 4. Temporary employees are all self-employed.

_____ 5. Businesses try to keep the size of their workforce small to save money.

_____ 6. If you have a college degree, learning on the job will not be important to you.

_____ 7. White male workers dominate the workforce in this country.

_____ 8. Teenagers will have little trouble getting hired for minimum-wage jobs.

_____ 9. Diversity in the workforce brings new ways to solve business problems.

_____10. Greater numbers of women in the workforce have brought positive changes in the way businesses view the families of both male and female workers.

Chapter 2 Test Questions

Part 1. Fill in the Blank

Fill in the missing word or words in each sentence.

1. A worker who is on time and at work every day is
   _____.

2. Business owners receive a _____ for risking their
   money in their companies.

3. Federal laws prevent an employer from _____ in any
   way because of race, gender, age, disability, national origin, or religion.

4. Laws require that employers make sure that workers wear
   _____ equipment such as hardhats and eye protectors
   in dangerous job conditions.

5. A _____ worker can be trusted to complete a job and
   find more work to do.

6. Businesses spend billions of dollars providing on-the-job
   _____ for employees.

7. Successful workers understand how to work effectively in
   _____ rather than just as individuals.

8. Profit-sharing programs offer a share of a business's profits to all
   _____ as a reward for their hard work.

9. Adaptive or _____ skills help employees adjust to the
   workplace.

10. Child labor laws prevent anyone under the age of 18 from working in a
    _____ job.

Part 2. Multiple Choice

Circle the letter that best completes each statement.

1. In states with right-to-work laws, workers

   a. must join the union at their place of employment.

   b. may refuse to join the union at their place of
      employment but must pay union dues.

   c. may choose to join any union in that state.

d. may refuse to join the union at their place of employment and not pay union dues.

e. may ask their employers to pay their union dues.

2. Before filing a complaint with a government agency concerning an employee rights issue, you should

   a. discuss the situation with your supervisor and ask for a correction.

   b. discuss the problem with the personnel office or the owner and ask for help in solving the problem.

   c. be sure you understand the situation fully.

   d. give your supervisor an opportunity to explain the problem.

   e. all of the above

3. An employer's profit is

   a. the money earned through sales and services.

   b. the income of the business minus the expenses of the business.

   c. the bills paid by the business.

   d. the money the employer invests in the business.

   e. the wages paid to new workers.

4. To compete in the world economy, businesses

   a. must provide a high-quality product or service.

   b. must pay workers the minimum wage.

   c. must hire younger workers.

   d. must require workers to join unions.

   e. must speed up production of products.

5. The minimum wage

   a. must be paid by all employers.

   b. is the same in every state.

   c. established by the federal government applies to most employers.

   d. is set by a panel of employers throughout the country.

   e. was lowered in 1996.

6. Child labor laws

    a. protect only those children under the age of 10.

    b. require employers to have proof of age from young workers.

    c. allow 15-year-olds to work in factories.

    d. require parents to provide work permits.

    e. limit the number of hours a 13-year-old may work.

7. Nonprofit agencies

    a. must provide services for less than the amount of their budgets.

    b. include many hospitals and social service agencies.

    c. may not distribute earnings greater than their expenses to stockholders.

    d. are expected to operate efficiently.

    e. all of the above

8. Federal and state laws governing employee safety

    a. have little to do with the work area.

    b. make workers responsible for their own safety.

    c. require that workers be taught what to do in case of being exposed to hazardous materials at work.

    d. allow 14-year-olds to work unlimited hours at any time of day or night.

    e. offer no help to employees working in unsafe conditions.

9. Laws concerning unfair dismissal of employees usually

    a. are very clear.

    b. are easily understood.

    c. are consistent throughout the country.

    d. require an attorney's opinion to be understood.

    e. make protesting an unfair dismissal speedy work.

10. Employers are looking for workers

    a. who work alone.

    b. who need no more learning experiences or training.

    c. who can read, write, compute, and communicate.

    d. who let others solve problems.

    e. who have no career goals.

Part 3. True or False

Read the following statements. Put a "T" beside each true statement and an "F" beside each false one.

_____ 1. Workers today need a higher level of skills than workers 20 years ago needed.

_____ 2. Employers want workers with self-esteem because they take pride in their work.

_____ 3. A profit-making company must work hard to satisfy its customers.

_____ 4. A perfect job is available for every employee.

_____ 5. You should always report each and every rule your employer does not obey.

_____ 6. There are no federal laws dealing with employee participation in union activity.

_____ 7. Never take a job that does not fully satisfy all of your job expectations.

_____ 8. Federal laws prohibit sexual harassment on the job.

_____ 9. You should file a complaint with a government agency about your employer only after careful consideration.

_____10. You need to learn how a business is organized to be an effective employee.

Chapter 3 Test Questions

Part 1. Fill in the Blank

Fill in the missing word or words in each sentence.

1. Health insurance, paid holidays, and low-cost child care are _____ employers may offer.

2. You may be offered the choice of being paid by check or _____ .

3. To learn how to dress correctly on your first day at work, ask your _____ .

4. Some employers pay college _____ for employees taking work-related courses.

5. In large organizations, new workers often report to the _____ office on their first workday.

6. A company may require you to take a _____ test as part of a physical exam.

7. _____ is the key to making your first day on the job a great one.

8. Call the personnel office to find out _____ to arrive, where to go, and who to contact on your first workday.

9. New workers often are required to attend _____ training to learn about the company and its policies.

10. At least 15 percent or more of your paycheck may be withheld for _____ and other deductions.

Part 2. Multiple Choice

Circle the letter that best completes each statement.

1. Workers at your new workplace wear uniforms. Before your first day on the job, you should

    a. go buy at least two uniforms.

    b. ask to borrow a uniform from another worker.

    c. ask your supervisor if you need a uniform the first day.

    d. wait for your supervisor to tell you what to do.

    e. none of the above

2. To legally work in this country, workers who are not citizens of the United States must

   a. take a drug test.

   b. show a copy of their birth certificate.

   c. pass a test on the Constitution of the United States.

   d. pay a labor permit tax.

   e. file an immigrant work authorization permit with their employer.

3. Employers offering a cafeteria plan of fringe benefits allow employees

   a. to eat free in the company lunchroom.

   b. to choose the fringe benefits that meet their needs.

   c. to have unlimited fringe benefits as long as they work for the company.

   d. to work in the company cafeteria to earn extra income.

   e. no fringe benefits.

4. To withhold taxes from your paycheck, your employer will need

   a. your Social Security number.

   b. your driver's license.

   c. your high school diploma.

   d. your birth certificate.

   e. all of the above

5. The most important person in your work life is

   a. the person who hires you.

   b. the person who makes out the payroll checks.

   c. your union representative.

   d. your supervisor.

   e. your coworker.

6. The telephone system at your workplace

   a. is not important to your job.

   b. should be used according to the company's procedures.

    c. should be used for your personal calls when you need to make them.

    d. should never be used by employees.

    e. should not be answered if your supervisor is not present.

7. On your first day of work your employer may ask you to bring

    a. your birth certificate.

    b. your Social Security card.

    c. your physical exam results.

    d. your driver's license.

    e. all of the above

8. Adjusting to your new job will be easier if

    a. you tell other workers how to do the job quicker.

    b. you ask the same questions each day.

    c. you keep your sense of humor and follow instructions.

    d. you keep quiet and don't ask questions.

    e. you keep to yourself and don't bother the other workers.

9. An important basic rule during the first few days on the job is

    a. avoid asking questions.

    b. don't worry about the way you are dressed.

    c. take as many breaks as possible.

    d. ask questions and remember the answers.

    e. ignore your coworkers.

10. Written company policy

    a. is rarely important.

    b. will not affect you.

    c. won't make any difference if you aren't aware of it.

    d. is just put together for public relations.

    e. should be read carefully.

Part 3. True or False

Read the following statements. Put a "T" beside each true statement and an "F" beside each false one.

_____ 1. A union may have an agreement with an employer to withhold union dues from payroll checks even from nonunion members.

_____ 2. If your employer offers a fringe benefit free of charge, you should sign up for it.

_____ 3. Your employer cannot require employee drug testing.

_____ 4. What you wear your first day on the job is not important.

_____ 5. If an occupational license is needed for your job, you will be expected to apply and pay for it.

_____ 6. All you need to do your first workday is get to the workplace on time.

_____ 7. New employees may not get paid on the first payday after starting work.

_____ 8. If you exceed the number of sick days you have earned you will not be paid for days you can't work because you are sick.

_____ 9. If you must pay part or all of the fringe benefit cost, you should only sign up for those benefits you need.

_____10. Your supervisor will have little effect on your work life.

Chapter 4 Test Questions

Part 1. Fill in the Blank

Fill in the missing word or words in the sentence.

1. The way you _____ and act will affect the way people treat you.

2. To avoid exposure to toxic fumes, many workers are required to wear _____ .

3. In many organizations, smoking is only allowed _____ the buildings.

4. Using words that are commonly understood rather than slang will make you appear bright and _____ .

5. Workers in _____ occupations are required to wash their hands before working with a patient.

6. _____ is personal body care.

7. In the last 10 years, dress for work has become more _____ .

8. If you are not sure how to dress for your job, the best way to find out is to _____ your supervisor.

9. If you refuse to wear safety equipment you may be _____ .

10. Avoid such _____ as pulling your ear or using slang.

Part 2. Multiple Choice

Circle the letter that best completes each statement.

1. Dressing appropriately means

    a. wearing a low-cut dress to work.

    b. all workers dress exactly the same.

    c. wearing jeans with holes.

    d. wearing clothing similar to that of your supervisor and coworkers.

    e. wearing an unbuttoned shirt.

2. Common safety equipment includes

    a. ear protectors, gloves, and safety glasses.

    b. athletic shoes, jeans, and jackets.

    c. uniforms, masks, and socks.

    d. hard hats, long chains, and sandals.

    e. loose clothing, boots, and aprons.

3. Body piercing

    a. is widely accepted in most jobs.

    b. is accepted equally for women and men.

    c. of the lips, eyebrows, or nose are less acceptable than of the ears.

    d. is not a hindrance in the workplace.

    e. is never appropriate in the workplace.

4. The way you dress

    a. has little to do with the way your supervisor views you.

    b. should make you stand out from your coworkers.

    c. may affect pay raises and promotions.

    d. should always be casual and comfortable.

    e. should express your individual personality.

5. Workers in food preparation services

    a. may wear aprons to prevent germs and dirt from getting into food.

    b. may wear plastic gloves to control the spread of germs into food.

    c. may wear hair nets on the job.

    d. should wash their hands with soap for 10-15 seconds after using the rest room.

    e. all of the above

6. Using a portable radio on the job

    a. is acceptable in all workplaces.

    b. will make your work time go faster.

    c. will impress your employer with your interest in your job.

d. may cause safety hazards in some workplaces.

e. will help you communicate with your coworkers.

7. Smokers

a. are free to smoke anywhere in most workplaces.

b. may work in smoke-free organizations.

c. are considered better workers than nonsmoking workers.

d. may use chewing tobacco or snuff as an acceptable alternative to smoking on the job.

e. create a positive image of themselves.

8. If you don't like your appearance, you should

a. wear brighter, more unique clothing.

b. accept the fact that you will never get ahead in your job.

c. do your best to look as good as possible and develop a good self-image and mental attitude.

d. recognize that you just aren't as good as your coworkers.

e. none of the above

9. Poor personal hygiene

a. can cause coworkers to complain about working with you.

b. has nothing to do with the workplace.

c. should never concern a supervisor.

d. has little affect on getting ahead on the job.

e. has no influence on customers.

10. Your boss and your coworkers will form an impression of you by

a. the way you speak.

b. the type clothing you wear.

c. the way you care for your body.

d. the way you style your hair.

e. all of the above

Part 3. True or False

*Read the following statements. Put a "T" beside each true statement
and an "F" beside each false one.*

_____ 1. Chewing gum distorts your facial expressions and makes it
hard to speak clearly.

_____ 2. Casual dress means wearing any type of clothing you have.

_____ 3. Being physically fit can help you do more work and lead to
promotions.

_____ 4. Employees working with hazardous materials are required
to provide their own protective clothing.

_____ 5. Wearing a mustache is acceptable in most jobs.

_____ 6. Official dress codes must be fair to all employees.

_____ 7. Refusing to wear safety equipment can mean losing your
job.

_____ 8. Using an expensive cologne always helps mask body odor
that may offend your coworkers.

_____ 9. Sometimes dress can be as important to job success as work
skills.

_____ 10. Some unofficial dress codes don't allow workers to wear
jeans or shorts.

Chapter 5 Test Questions

Part 1. Fill in the Blank

Fill in the missing word or words in each sentence.

1. Recording your work schedule and personal appointments in a _____ will help you plan your life.

2. To avoid missing work, try to schedule personal _____ outside of regular work time.

3. You can reduce the amount of _____ in your life by practicing good health habits.

4. The amount of sleep you get affects your _____ level.

5. The way you live your life from day-to-day is your _____ .

6. _____ with other workers saves money and is a reliable way to get to work each day.

7. Employee absence costs a business _____ .

8. If you are not able to get to work, _____ your supervisor as soon as possible.

9. Planning to get to work 8 to 10 minutes early will help you avoid being _____ .

10. A _____ is a child, an elderly adult, or a person with disabilities who lives in your home and is supported financially by you.

Part 2. Multiple Choice

Circle the letter that best completes each statement.

1. Getting to work on time

    a. will not influence your employer.

    b. is not important if you are less than 15 minutes late.

    c. will positively influence your supervisor's evaluation of you.

    d. is not expected if you have young children.

    e. will not affect your pay.

2. Employee absence affects

    a. supervisors.

    b. promotions.

    c. customer satisfaction.

    d. coworkers.

    e. all of the above

3. Friday/Monday Syndrome

    a. is a pattern of employee absences on Mondays and Fridays.

    b. is a rare disease that occurs only on Mondays and Fridays.

    c. is a legitimate reason for an extended weekend holiday.

    d. rarely appears in younger employees.

    e. is not irritating to supervisors.

4. If you are sick and cannot get to work, you should

    a. go back to sleep and not worry about work.

    b. tell someone in your carpool to tell your boss you are sick.

    c. not worry about contacting your supervisor.

    d. call your supervisor as soon as possible to explain why you can't get to work.

    e. just wait and apologize to your supervisor when you get back at work.

5. When employees are absent, businesses lose money because

    a. employees received "docked" pay.

    b. other employees don't work as hard.

    c. it's hard to produce as many goods.

    d. nobody knows what to do without the absent employee.

    e. other employees leave the workplace.

6. Good customer service

    a. is not a concern for American business.

    b. encourages people to return to the business and buy more.

    c. has nothing to do with workers.

    d. is provided only by management workers.

    e. is not affected by employee absence.

7. Your coworkers

    a. will not be affected if you miss work.

    b. are an excellent source of romantic relationships.

    c. should be among your closest friends.

    d. always expect you to take sides in a dispute with the supervisor.

    e. should never be your friends.

8. As a working parent, you should

    a. expect your supervisor to help you find emergency child care.

    b. never use newspaper ads to hire a baby-sitter.

    c. have at least two dependable people to call for emergency child care.

    d. leave your child at home alone when the daycare center closes for bad weather.

    e. send your sick child to school and let the school nurse handle the problem.

9. To schedule vacations, you should

    a. find out when other workers are taking vacations.

    b. talk to your supervisor to find out what needs to be done.

    c. ask for the time off your first day on the job.

    d. on Tuesday tell your supervisor you are taking two weeks off starting Thursday.

    e. call your boss from Florida and say you'll be back a week from Friday.

10. Dependable workers

    a. cause problems for their coworkers.

    b. plan ahead and prepare for emergencies.

    c. are just born organized.

    d. never, ever miss work.

    e. don't have the same problems undependable workers have.

Part 3. True or False

Read the following statements. Put a "T" beside each true statement and an "F" beside each false one.

_____ 1. A business can't reduce a worker's paycheck because of tardiness.

_____ 2. One in four employers would hire a nonsmoker rather than an equally qualified smoker.

_____ 3. Staying up late and getting up early will not affect your work.

_____ 4. Spending time in jail can mean losing your job.

_____ 5. Lying to your supervisor can get you fired.

_____ 6. Arriving at work 8 to 10 minutes early will help reduce stress and prepare you for the workday.

_____ 7. Tardy workers have little affect on a supervisor's workday.

_____ 8. Your work should be your social life.

_____ 9. Avoiding excesses will make your life less stressful.

_____10. Most employers are not concerned about drug use on the job.

Chapter 6 Test Questions

Part 1. Fill in the Blank

Fill in the missing word or words in each sentence.

1. To learn how to do your job and what your supervisor expects, talk to your _____ .

2. Your _____ is the way you prefer to learn.

3. Adults learn best by _____ the task.

4. Time and _____ are needed to learn a new skill.

5. To learn about the responsibilities and tasks involved with your job, ask your supervisor to explain or give you a job _____ .

6. One-on-one instruction that takes place as you work is _____ training.

7. A _____ project is the way you learn something new.

8. The more you practice a _____ you have learned, the more productive you become.

9. Completing the _____ is the most important step in a learning project.

10. To keep your _____ job skills up-to-date, you will need to be responsible for your learning.

Part 2. Multiple Choice

Circle the letter that best completes each statement.

1. The two basic types of training employers use are

   a. lectures and conferences.

   b. private training companies and college courses.

   c. on-the-job training and classroom instruction.

   d. videos and vocational schools.

   e. continuing education courses at high schools and colleges.

2. Adults learn best when

   a. learning is very structured.

   b. another person demonstrates a skill.

c. someone tells them how to do a task.

d. they listen to a lecture.

e. they perform the task.

3. Your supervisor

    a. will not be involved in your training.

    b. will expect you to ask questions about your new job.

    c. will expect you to listen and not ask questions.

    d. will expect you to start your new job with no instruction.

    e. will not evaluate your work skills.

4. On-the-job training

    a. is usually one-on-one training.

    b. may be given by a supervisor or a coworker.

    c. takes place as a new worker does the job.

    d. allows the new worker to practice the job.

    e. all of the above

5. Workshops offered by private training companies

    a. are never worth the money.

    b. are difficult to find.

    c. will meet your learning style.

    d. vary greatly in quality.

    e. are offered for low fees.

6. Your education

    a. is complete when you receive a college degree.

    b. should be your employer's responsibility.

    c. has no affect on your earnings.

    d. should continue throughout your lifetime.

    e. should be limited to formal schooling.

7. Your coworkers

    a. may help you learn how to please your supervisor.

    b. should never be used to learn new job skills.

    c. are never involved in on-the-job training.

d. are not helpful in learning how to do your job.

e. should be ignored until you learn your job.

8. Your learning style

 a. is not important on the job.

 b. has no affect when you are learning a new task.

 c. is the way you learn most effectively.

 d. changes often.

 e. should be the only way you are willing to learn.

9. A learning project

 a. does not involve motivating yourself.

 b. is a plan to learn something new.

 c. should not have a completion date.

 d. requires your supervisor's written permission.

 e. does not need any objectives.

10. Lifelong learning

 a. means taking college courses every five years.

 b. does not affect your earning power.

 c. does not interest businesses.

 d. is geared for people over 65.

 e. is the key to success in the new labor market.

Part 3. True or False

Read the following statements. Put a "T" beside each true statement and an "F" beside each false one.

_____ 1. All learning is completed in a structured manner.

_____ 2. Knowing your learning style will help you learn better.

_____ 3. Knowing how to learn is the most important skill you can have.

_____ 4. When you have learned a skill you no longer need to practice it.

_____ 5. Successful learning means setting objectives and accomplishing them.

_____ 6. If you are forced to use a learning method you do not prefer, you can temporarily adopt another learning style.

_____ 7. Adults do not need a reason to learn.

_____ 8. Some employers will pay for courses offered through adult education programs.

_____ 9. Your college degree means you do not need any more job training.

_____10. Using your local library can help you learn about your new occupation.

Chapter 7 Test Questions

Part 1. Fill in the Blank

Fill in the missing word or words in each sentence.

1. You must _____ you can do a job to actually do it.

2. Employers want workers with _____ skills, such as getting to work on time, being honest, and getting the job done.

3. People with _____ believe they can do their jobs.

4. Self-image is the way you see _____ .

5. _____ with your supervisor, coworkers, and customers is important to your job success.

6. You are responsible for your successes and your _____, but people and events can affect your life.

7. People with _____ self-concepts believe luck is responsible for their failures.

8. Question yourself in order to _____ your abilities.

9. Operating a forklift is an example of a _____ skill.

10. Managing people is a _____ skill that can be used in many different jobs.

Part 2. Multiple Choice

Circle the letter that best completes each statement.

1. The most important influence in forming your self-image is

   a. your parents.

   b. you.

   c. your peers.

   d. your siblings.

   e. your teacher.

2. Job-related skills

   a. must be learned in technical schools.

   b. are learned through both education and life experience.

c. are never learned on the job.

d. have nothing to do with your life interests.

e. will not affect your ability to do a new job.

3. When you make a mistake on the job, you should

    a. avoid talking to your supervisor.

    b. keep blaming yourself.

    c. quit your job.

    d. decide the job is too difficult for you.

    e. try to learn how to improve.

4. A worker with a positive self-concept

    a. is motivated.

    b. produces better quality work.

    c. will experience job success.

    d. will have high morale.

    e. all of the above

5. Self-awareness

    a. has nothing to do with your self-concept.

    b. makes you appear as a "know-it-all."

    c. means you understand your strengths and weaknesses.

    d. means you will always be confident.

    e. can accomplished only be through meditation.

6. People with positive self-concepts

    a. believe in pure luck.

    b. blame others for their failures.

    c. never question their abilities.

    d. accept control of their lives.

    e. all of the above

7. To protect your positive self-image at a new job, you should

    a. ignore any criticism from your boss.

    b. remember you can be fired for any reason.

    c. realize your employer wants you to be a success.

    d. never admit making a mistake.

    e. remember you are on probation.

8. Self-management skills

    a. are not useful in the workplace.

    b. help you be punctual, dependable, and reliable.

    c. are rarely used on the job.

    d. have no affect on your job success.

    e. do not help you get a job.

9. You can choose

    a. the way your supervisor treats you.

    b. what your friends say about you.

    c. how your teacher evaluates you.

    d. to know and value yourself.

    e. how your family sees you.

10. When you are praised by your supervisor, you should

    a. respond by saying "Thank you."

    b. tell your coworkers.

    c. ignore the compliment.

    d. tell your supervisor you don't deserve the praise.

    e. say nothing.

Part 3. True or False

Read the following statements. Put a "T" beside each true statement and an "F" beside each false one.

_____ 1. Transferable skills can be used in many different jobs.

_____ 2. People with self-confidence never question their job skills.

_____ 3. Success and failure at work is a matter of luck.

_____ 4. Knowing your job skills will help you earn promotions and raises.

_____ 5. Getting along with coworkers is a transferable skill.

_____ 6. Your parents are responsible for your self-image.

_____ 7. Employers typically look for reasons to fire new employees.

_____ 8. Admitting a mistake on the job is not wise.

_____ 9. Believing in yourself is necessary for success on the job.

_____10. Everyone can experience a poor self-image during times of change.

Chapter 8 Test Questions

Part 1. Fill in the Blank

Fill in the missing word or words in each sentence.

1. Asking _____ can help you avoid making mistakes on the job.

2. A worker's job performance is evaluated using a performance _____ .

3. In order to get work done, a supervisor _____ tasks to workers.

4. The official procedure for resolving a conflict with a supervisor is called a _____ procedure.

5. During the _____ period a new employee should be very careful to follow the supervisor's instructions.

6. _____ action—such as being warned or suspended—may be taken if a worker's behavior is unacceptable.

7. Special terminology or abbreviations used within a company is called the company's _____ .

8. When a worker is _____ by a business as a disciplinary action, the worker often is not paid for three to five days while off work.

9. The added responsibilities of a supervisor can cause a great deal of _____ .

10. If a worker is fired, it is recorded permanently in the worker's _____ record .

Part 2. Multiple Choice

Circle the letter that best completes each statement.

1. When you are being trained, you should

   a. wait to ask questions until the end of the day.

   b. not hesitate to ask the same question several times.

   c. just listen and keep quiet.

   d. trust your supervisor to know what you don't understand.

   e. ask for clarification if you don't understand any instructions.

2. If the machine you are using to do your work is not working correctly, you should

    a. talk to your coworkers.

    b. contact your supervisor immediately.

    c. stop working and take a break.

    d. ignore the problem.

    e. just keep working.

3. If your supervisor angrily shouts at you, you should

    a. shout back.

    b. file a grievance.

    c. stay calm.

    d. quit your job.

    e. just walk out the door for the day.

4. If the telephone rings when your supervisor is gone, you should

    a. answer the phone, write down the message, and make sure your supervisor gets the information.

    b. tell the caller to call back later.

    c. not answer the telephone.

    d. memorize the message.

    e. tell the caller that answering the telephone is not your job.

5. If your supervisor compliments you, you should

    a. giggle and say you were just doing your job.

    b. make sure your coworkers hear about it.

    c. accept the praise and say "Thank you."

    d. say nothing.

    e. turn and walk away.

6. Workers who extend their break times

    a. don't affect the customers.

    b. are just doing what their supervisors expect.

    c. are exercising their personal rights.

    d. may cause other workers to miss their breaks.

    e. don't cause any problems on the job.

7. If you have a disagreement with your supervisor, you should

    a. immediately file a grievance with management.

    b. quit your job.

    c. take a few days off and look for another job.

    d. talk to your supervisor and try to work out a compromise.

    e. keep quiet and keep working.

8. During the probationary period, a worker

    a. may be fired without warning.

    b. must be warned twice before being dismissed.

    c. may not work overtime.

    d. has the same rights as any employee.

    e. will not be evaluated in any way.

9. When a job is delegated to you,

    a. you are expected to get the job done.

    b. you are expected to report the progress of the job to your supervisor.

    c. your supervisor is trusting you to do the work.

    d. your supervisor will expect to know when you have finished the job.

    e. all of the above

10. A supervisor

    a. never has to do the same work as other workers.

    b. can take a day off whenever he or she wants.

    c. is the team leader.

    d. has no influence in raises and promotions.

    e. all of the above

Part 3. True or False

Read the following statements. Put a "T" beside each true statement and an "F" beside each false one.

_____ 1. Keeping a notebook of job instructions will help you remember how to do certain jobs without asking your supervisor.

_____ 2. If you get your work done, you should wait for your supervisor to check on you before doing another job.

_____ 3. A supervisor's job is not complicated or stressful.

_____ 4. If you are not sure what your supervisor thinks of your work, you should ask for feedback.

_____ 5. If your supervisor leaves for the afternoon, it's okay to leave work early.

_____ 6. New employees must learn to work as quickly as possible while still doing a quality job.

_____ 7. Not every supervisor offers employees feedback about their work.

_____ 8. You are not expected to take telephone messages.

_____ 9. Practicing a task will help you know what your supervisor expects.

_____10. If you don't understand a term used by your supervisor, it is best to ignore what was said.

Chapter 9 Test Questions

Part 1. Fill in the Blank

Fill in the missing word or words in each sentence.

1. Following _____, such as ordering pizza the last Friday of each month, will help you become part of the team.

2. Voice mail, fax machines, e-mail, and computers require you to practice _____ etiquette in the workplace.

3. Violent threats to a supervisor or other workers are reasons for _____ an employee.

4. Your supervisor will evaluate your ability to be a part of the work _____ .

5. A work team is _____ when its members have different values and temperaments.

6. _____ means that a team working together can do more than the same number of people working individually.

7. Using another worker's computer without asking is an invasion of _____ .

8. Personal _____ are the importance we give to ideas, things, or people.

9. Individual _____ in a work team provides different viewpoints in finding solutions to problems.

10. Repeatedly asking another worker for a date after being turned down is _____ harassment.

Part 2. Multiple Choice

Circle the letter that best completes each statement.

1. The three basic ways people differ are

   a. age, values, and religion.

   b. culture, genetic structure, and age.

   c. facial features, blood type, and temperament.

   d. values, temperament, and individual characteristics.

   e. gender, blood type, and ethnicity.

2. To fit into the work team, you should

    a. accept racial harassment.

    b. find out what other workers expect from the newest member of the team.

    c. do another worker's job as well as your own.

    d. join the other workers in telling sexual jokes at break.

    e. expect the group to accept you right away.

3. Personal values

    a. have no affect on your work.

    b. of all team members should be the same.

    c. are either right or wrong.

    d. are the importance we give to ideas, things, or people.

    e. are useless in a work team.

4. If two coworkers are having a conflict, you should

    a. act as a sounding board for their frustrations.

    b. tell your supervisor about the problem.

    c. let them work out the problem.

    d. decide who is right and defend that person.

    e. offer to act as mediator in solving the problem.

5. Voice mail greetings should

    a. be unique.

    b. be personal.

    c. keep the caller entertained for a few moments.

    d. be short but informative.

    e. be musical.

6. Dating a coworker

    a. may cause stress at work.

    b. is accepted by all business organizations.

    c. will not affect other workers' attitudes toward you.

    d. will not affect your concentration at work.

    e. is the best way to get to know coworkers.

7. If you are threatened with violence by a coworker, you should

    a. avoid that person as much as possible.

    b. tell your supervisor.

    c. be understanding of that person's problems.

    d. threaten that person.

    e. carry a weapon to work.

8. Voice mail messages

    a. should be detailed.

    b. should express your anger if you are unhappy.

    c. should be short and give essentials.

    d. are useless in the business world.

    e. are a helpful way to discuss problems.

9. Temperament styles

    a. differ little from one person to another.

    b. are based on gender.

    c. are based on a person's race.

    d. never cause conflicts between individuals.

    e. affect the way people think, feel, and react to the world.

10. Diversity in the workforce

    a. will continue to be an important characteristic of the U.S. labor market.

    b. will weaken the team approach.

    c. will leave younger workers without jobs.

    d. will not affect the way problems are approached.

    e. will mean fewer women will be working full-time.

Part 3. True or False

Read the following statements. Put a "T" beside each true statement and an "F" beside each false one.

_____ 1. Reading a fax sent to another person is an acceptable workplace practice.

_____ 2. Employers are required by law to protect employees from sexual harassment.

_____ 3. You should tell your supervisor if another worker threatens you.

_____ 4. Doing a coworker's job will gain the respect of the other workers and of your supervisor.

_____ 5. Individual diversity on a work team can affect the way the team approaches problems.

_____ 6. Being honest will help you gain the respect of your coworkers.

_____ 7. Your coworkers will want to know how great your old job was.

_____ 8. Other workers' computers and floppy disks are considered private.

_____ 9. An optimist and a realist can never work together successfully.

_____10. Gossiping is a good way to find out about your coworkers.

Chapter 10 Test Questions

Part 1. Fill in the Blank

Fill in the missing word or words in each sentence.

1. Balancing the needs of several customers at the same time is a good customer service _____ .

2. If employees are not interested in serving customers, the business will _____ customers.

3. As an employee, your first and most important job is _____ customers.

4. Good _____ skills include looking at the customer, nodding, not interrupting, and being attentive.

5. A _____ such as "Hello, may I help you?" lets a customer know you are interested and ready to help.

6. Good customer service begins with your _____ .

7. You can create a customer who is a fan by giving them a _____ along with everything they expect.

8. Good _____ is treating customers the way that you would like to be treated.

9. Poor service, a faulty product, or dissatisfaction with a product can result in a customer _____ .

10. If a customer is angry or rude, you may need to get help from your _____ .

Part 2. Multiple Choice

Circle the letter that best completes each statement.

1. When dealing with a rude customer, you should

   a. tolerate the rudeness.

   b. ignore the customer and help a different customer.

   c. be rude back.

   d. ask how you can help and provide the best possible service.

   e. call the police.

2. According to one study, businesses lose customers most often because

   a. prices are too high.

   b. friends recommend a different business.

   c. employees do not offer good customer service.

   d. customers move.

   e. a new business opens.

3. If you are helping a customer and another customer comes into the store, you should

   a. leave the first customer immediately.

   b. ignore the second customer until the first customer leaves.

   c. keep working with the first customer and let the second customer browse without interruption.

   d. tell the second customer you will help him or her as soon as you finish with the first customer.

   e. let the customers handle their own problems.

4. If a business telephone is not answered promptly

   a. the customer knows all the employees are busy.

   b. business will not be affected.

   c. customers will understand.

   d. the telephone company will charge extra for excessive ringing.

   e. customers will hang up.

5. Good customer service

   a. is not important if you work in a government agency.

   b. is the most important task of an employee.

   c. has little affect on customer satisfaction.

   d. does not affect a company's profits.

   e. will not affect a customer's loyalty.

6. Customers

   a. never cause interruptions for workers.

   b. always express their wants clearly.

   c. do not expect friendliness in a business setting.

d. are important to business because they buy products or services.

e. expect to wait while an employee talks on the phone.

7. When a customer is angry, you should

   a. take a break.

   b. ignore him or her and walk away.

   c. pretend you don't notice the anger.

   d. respond by being angry.

   e. offer to help correct the situation that has caused the anger.

8. When you are resolving a customer complaint, you should

   a. clearly tell the customer how the problem will be solved.

   b. not be concerned about understanding the complaint.

   c. ignore the customer.

   d. give the customer whatever he or she wants.

   e. not worry about contacting the customer after finding a solution to the problem.

9. When taking a phone message, you should

   a. not ask for the correct spelling of the caller's name, because that's rude.

   b. tell the caller exactly what the employee is doing for the day.

   c. tell the caller to just call back tomorrow.

   d. tell the caller to expect a return call at 3:30 Friday afternoon.

   e. ask to take a message and deliver it when the employee returns.

10. The way a customer is treated

   a. makes a difference in the way a customer treats the employee.

   b. determines if the customer buys a business's product or service.

   c. determines the way a customer thinks about a business.

   d. determines if the customer returns to buy more.

   e. all of the above

Part 3. True or False

Read the following statements. Put a "T" beside each true statement and an "F" beside each false one.

_____ 1. Talking to a customer on the telephone is more important than helping a customer who is in the business place.

_____ 2. Customers buying a product or service are satisfied by price, quality, and customer service.

_____ 3. Listening to a customer includes looking at him or her, smiling, and nodding.

_____ 4. Asking customers questions only confuses them.

_____ 5. Putting a telephone customer on hold should be avoided.

_____ 6. Your supervisor's help may be needed when an angry customer refuses to be calmed.

_____ 7. Making a customer feel happy is not an employee's job.

_____ 8. Interrupting a customer with questions helps to quickly find out what he or she wants.

_____ 9. Understanding what a customer wants is an important step in providing customer satisfaction.

_____10. Customers expect employees to provide information about products and services.

Chapter 11 Test Questions

Part 1. Fill in the Blank

Fill in the missing word or words in each sentence.

1. Employees are assuming responsibilities once performed by _____ .

2. To avoid working on the wrong problem, you should first _____ the problem.

3. The ability to think of new ideas or apply old ideas to solve new problems is being _____ .

4. To select the number one idea from a large number of ideas, use both _____ and _____ .

5. Reading _____ or magazines about a certain type of business will help you learn about problem-solving in your field.

6. Organizing data about a problem to find a solution is called _____ .

7. Employees who develop _____ skills are valued members of the work team.

8. Employees who are involved in solving problems are more _____ to do a better job.

9. Managers relying on employees and work teams to solve problems is called employee _____ .

10. A group of employees brought together to solve problems is sometimes called a _____ circle.

Part 2. Multiple Choice

Circle the letter that best completes each statement.

1. Employees often are able to find solutions to problems

   a. faster than managers.

   b. because they are more creative than managers.

   c. because they are closer to most problems than managers and supervisors.

   d. less often than managers.

   e. very rarely.

2. Problem solving

    a. is not valued by businesses.

    b. is not organized in any form.

    c. can be approached in any order.

    d. is a highly marketable skill.

    e. is used only by managers and supervisors.

3. Brainstorming

    a. is a forum for a group of workers to complain about their supervisor.

    b. is a way to come up with as many ideas to solve a problem as possible.

    c. is useful for an individual studying problems.

    d. focuses on a few, limited ways to solve problems.

    e. none of the above

4. To analyze data you can use

    a. time tables and mathematical tables.

    b. word processing programs on a computer.

    c. information found on the Internet.

    d. frequency tables, percentages, and graphs.

    e. the nominal group technique.

5. In order to solve a problem,

    a. you must have a college education.

    b. you must know what the problem is.

    c. you don't need to believe that a solution exists.

    d. you should work alone.

    e. reading will not be helpful.

6. Creative thinking in solving problems should

    a. include looking at the problem from different viewpoints.

    b. always use a serious approach.

    c. always use a specific, literal plan.

    d. be done quickly.

    e. be done in a busy environment.

7. Employees are needed to solve problems

    a. as the number of managers and supervisors increases.

    b. as businesses become simpler to operate.

    c. as more employees assume responsibilities once performed by managers.

    d. as supervisors make more complex decisions.

    e. as technology creates a simpler form of business.

8. In a group discussion using the nominal group technique

    a. each person thinks of as many ideas as possible and writes out each idea.

    b. the group shares ideas from each person in a round-robin manner.

    c. the group discusses each idea.

    d. the group ranks the ideas from best to worst.

    e. all of the above

9. A quality circle is

    a. the area of a business where new products are tested.

    b. used to rate employees' work.

    c. no longer a relevant part of the business world.

    d. a way to teach supervisors management skills.

    e. a group of employees who meet in order to identify problems and find solutions.

10. Analysis is

    a. observing what is happening in a problem situation.

    b. talking to people about the problem.

    c. organizing data to find a solution to a problem.

    d. gathering data.

    e. all of the above

Part 3. True or False

Read the following statements. Put a "T" beside each true statement and an "F" beside each false one.

_____ 1. A solution's cost is not important when solving a problem.

_____ 2. Seeking solutions from other parts of the business or from other organizations is wise.

_____ 3. If a solution to a problem does not work the first time, you should find a different solution.

_____ 4. Creativity involves finding new ideas and using old ideas to solve new problems.

_____ 5. Relaxing can help you discover new solutions for problems.

_____ 6. One form of employee involvement is using work teams to solve problems on the job.

_____ 7. Knowing how to implement the solution to a problem is not as important as finding an immediate solution.

_____ 8. The best solution to the problem is the first idea that comes to mind.

_____ 9. Identifying the real problem is the first step in the problem-solving process.

_____10. Rating and ranking are two ways to select the best solution from a list of many.

Chapter 12 Test Questions

Part 1. Fill in the Blank

Fill in the missing word or words in each sentence.

1. _____ behavior on the job costs businesses billions of dollars each year.

2. Local, state, and federal _____ express the ethical behavior expected of everyone in society.

3. Copying software illegally is called _____ .

4. The principles or standards that govern our behavior are called _____ .

5. Company trade secrets and private information about customers and employees are _____ and should not be shared without permission.

6. Many businesses provide a _____ that lists the personnel regulations governing its employees' behavior.

7. When employees copy software _____ the employer can be sued.

8. A good _____ helps people choose to do the right thing, even under pressure.

9. Using recreational drugs on the job can result in immediate _____ .

10. Most people learn ethical behavior while they're growing up and continue using the same ethics as _____ .

Part 2. Multiple Choice

Circle the letter that best completes each statement.

1. If your supervisor tells you to do something illegal,

    a. you don't need to be concerned.

    b. you should follow your supervisor's instructions without question.

    c. you will not be accountable for any illegal action.

    d. you are still legally responsible for your actions.

    e. you may protect yourself by claiming ignorance of the law.

2. Making personal long-distance telephone calls using the company's telephone system

   a. is a fringe benefit you should expect from your employer.

   b. doesn't cost the company much money.

   c. is one of the most expensive crimes in business.

   d. will cost less since telephone rates during the business day are so low.

   e. will not irritate your supervisor.

3. Substance abuse on the job

   a. will not affect your job status.

   b. results in lower productivity.

   c. is not a concern of employers.

   d. has no affect on accident rates on the job.

   e. cannot be a reason for your job termination.

4. Employees having access to confidential information

   a. need to know the organization's policy on confidentiality.

   b. are not responsible if trade secrets are shared.

   c. cannot harm the company by revealing information.

   d. cannot affect the reputation of other employees.

   e. cannot reveal any data that would aid a competitor.

5. A coworker's unethical behavior should be reported to the supervisor

   a. when you hear gossip about it at your break time.

   b. when another coworker tells you at the company party.

   c. only after you have told other coworkers.

   d. when you see the employee engage in it.

   e. only if you want to impress your supervisor.

6. When you are trying to make an ethical decision, you should follow this guideline:

   a. if it is legal, do it.

   b. if you will gain, do it.

   c. if your supervisor advises, do it.

d. if it improves your self-esteem, do it.

e. use as many principles as you can apply to make the decision.

7. New workers need to know

    a. how employee discounts are used.

    b. how to extend their break times.

    c. how to make personal long-distance phone calls using the company phone system.

    d. how to avoid working a full day.

    e. how to make copies for personal use.

8. Commercial software

    a. may be copied without any restrictions.

    b. may be shared with company employees for personal use.

    c. may be copied and sold to anyone working for the business.

    d. is protected by copyright laws.

    e. may be copied as long as it is not sold to anyone else.

9. Ethics

    a. are principles that govern our behavior.

    b. usually are learned as we grow up.

    c. may differ among supervisors and workers.

    d. guide people in their daily actions.

    e. all of the above

10. Practicing unethical behavior

    a. does not affect a worker's job status.

    b. can result in disciplinary action.

    c. does not cause problems on the job.

    d. does not affect a worker's job success.

    e. does not cost a business anything.

Part 3. True or False

Read the following statements. Put a "T" beside each true statement and an "F" beside each false one.

_____ 1. Ethical decisions are not always strictly right or wrong.

_____ 2. All moral people share the same ethical principles.

_____ 3. Laws express the ethical behaviors expected of everyone in society.

_____ 4. People in authority always support ethical behavior.

_____ 5. Using the company's photocopier for personal use is accepted as an employee benefit.

_____ 6. If you hear about another employee's unethical behavior, you should report it to your supervisor.

_____ 7. Using drugs or alcohol on the job can result in immediate termination.

_____ 8. Leaving the job early or arriving to work late is stealing time from an employer.

_____ 9. Employees who disobey the personnel policies of a company usually are disciplined.

_____10. Drug use on the job can be a safety hazard.

Chapter 13 Test Questions

Part 1. Fill in the Blank

Fill in the missing word or words in each sentence.

1. The amount of time a person has worked at a job is called
   _____ .

2. The quality of a person's job performance is called
   _____ .

3. Both seniority and merit are considered when deciding which employees
   will be _____ .

4. The process of reaching your personal goals in work and life is termed
   _____ development.

5. A _____ is a flat payment received each week or
   month, regardless of the number of hours worked.

6. A _____ is a specific amount of money earned for
   each hour a person works.

7. A person who takes a long-term interest in another worker and offers advice
   about advancing on the job is a _____ .

8. Typically, an employee is expected to give a notice of
   _____ two weeks before leaving the job.

9. A pay raise based on the inflation rate is called a _____
   increase.

10. In many companies, a job _____ notifies employees
    of a job vacancy.

Part 2. Multiple Choice

Circle the letter that best completes each statement.

1. A portfolio

   a. is a group of photographs showing you and your coworkers
      on the job.

   b. is your career plan.

   c. is the responsibility of the Human Resources Department of
      your employer.

d. is a record of skills you acquire, classes you attend, and projects or ideas you have submitted in your workplace.

e. is your high school records.

2. Pay raises

a. are used to keep valued employees.

b. may be given at the end of a worker's successful training period.

c. may be a part of a worker's promotion.

d. may be given to help employees offset inflation.

e. all of the above

3. A mentor

a. should be someone outside your workplace.

b. should be a family member.

c. is someone who takes a professional interest in you and advises you about your job.

d. does not need to understand your career plans.

e. all of the above

4. If you are dissatisfied with your job, you should

a. quit your job and look for another one.

b. tell your supervisor exactly why you are dissatisfied and quit.

c. quit your job immediately.

d. find another job and then tell your supervisor you are quitting.

e. tell your coworkers about your dissatisfaction before you leave.

5. After being on the job a few months, new workers typically are concerned about

a. overtime, sexual harassment, and raises.

b. raises, promotions, and downsizing.

c. promotions, job security, and vacation time.

d. health insurance, raises, and child care issues.

e. none of the above

6. Promotions

    a. are available only to people with many years of seniority.

    b. usually are not based on a worker's job skills.

    c. are based on seniority, merit, and job skills or knowledge.

    d. are given automatically after a year on the job.

    e. all of the above

7. Developing a career plan

    a. requires a professional career counselor's guidance.

    b. is not important for new workers.

    c. will help you reach your goals.

    d. should be done only once at the start of your career.

    e. is not your responsibility.

8. When you want a promotion you should

    a. always look outside your organization.

    b. contact the personnel office to learn about job openings.

    c. keep quiet and wait for your supervisor to promote you.

    d. count on your work record to bring it about.

    e. find as many ways as possible to learn about job vacancies in your organization.

9. To be prepared to get the best possible job today, you should

    a. emphasize your skills.

    b. keep a record of your accomplishments.

    c. learn new skills.

    d. get more experience and education.

    e. all of the above

10. Probation

    a. usually lasts two weeks.

    b. is considered a training period.

    c. has no affect on pay raises.

    d. is used only for poor employees.

    e. all of the above

Part 3. True or False

Read the following statements. Put a "T" beside each true statement and an "F" beside each false one.

_____ 1. Cost-of-living pay increases help workers offset inflation.

_____ 2. Learning new skills has little influence on raises and promotions.

_____ 3. Building a network is useful primarily for learning company gossip.

_____ 4. If someone with less seniority than you gets a promotion, you should ask why.

_____ 5. You should take charge of your own career development.

_____ 6. The average person changes careers five to seven times in his or her working life.

_____ 7. When you leave a job you should be sure your supervisor understands what you believe is wrong with the company.

_____ 8. A portfolio is not important when you are applying for a promotion.

_____ 9. Once you have set your career goals, you should never change them.

_____10. Incentive raises are based on evaluations and job performance.

Question Bank Answers

Answers for Chapter 1

Part 1. Fill in the Blank

1. workforce	6. temporary
2. ethnic	7. Core
3. family friendly	8. more
4. minimum	9. Diversity
5. Education	10. service

Part 2. Multiple Choice

1. E   2. C   3. A   4. D   5. E   6. C   7. B   8. C   9. A   10. D

Part 3. True or False

1. T   2. T   3. F   4. F   5. T   6. F   7. F   8. T   9. T   10. T

Answers for Chapter 2

Part 1. Fill in the Blank

1. dependable
2. profit
3. discriminating
4. safety
5. reliable
6. training
7. teams
8. employees
9. self-management
10. hazardous

Part 2. Multiple Choice

1. D 2. E 3. B 4. A 5. C 6. B 7. E 8. C 9. D 10. C

Part 3. True or False

1. T 2. T 3. T 4. F 5. F 6. F 7. F 8. T 9. T 10. T

Answers for Chapter 3

Part 1. Fill in the Blank

1. fringe benefits
2. direct deposit
3. supervisor
4. tuition
5. personnel or human resources
6. drug
7. Preparation
8. when
9. orientation
10. taxes

Part 2. Multiple Choice

1. C 2. E 3. B 4. A 5. D 6. B 7. E 8. C 9. D 10. E

Part 3. True or False

1. T 2. T 3. F 4. F 5. T 6. F 7. T 8. T 9. T 10. F

Answers for Chapter 4

Part 1. Multiple Choice

1. look
2. masks
3. outside
4. educated
5. health
6. Hygiene
7. casual
8. ask
9. fired
10. mannerisms

Part 2. Multiple Choice

1. D 2. A 3. C 4. C 5. E 6. D 7. B 8. C 9. A 10. E

Part 3. True or False

1. T 2. F 3. T 4. F 5. T 6. T 7. T 8. F 9. T 10. T

Answers for Chapter 5

Part 1. Fill in the Blank

1. calendar	6. Carpooling
2. appointments or business	7. money
3. stress	8. call
4. energy	9. late
5. lifestyle	10. dependent

Part 2. Multiple Choice

1. C   2. E   3. A   4. D   5. C   6. B   7. C   8. C   9. B   10. B

Part 3. True or False

1. F   2. T   3. F   4. T   5. T   6. T   7. F   8. F   9. T   10. F

Answers for Chapter 6

Part 1. Fill in the Blank

1. coworkers	6. on-the-job
2. learning style	7. learning
3. doing	8. skill
4. practice	9. objectives
5. description	10. lifelong

Part 2. Multiple Choice

1. C   2. E   3. B   4. E   5. D   6. D   7. A   8. C   9. B   10. E

Part 3. True or False

1. F   2. T   3. T   4. F   5. T   6. T   7. F   8. T   9. F   10. T

Answers for Chapter 7

Part 1. Fill in the Blank

1. believe	6. failures
2. self-management	7. poor
3. self-confidence	8. evaluate
4. yourself	9. job-related
5. Communicating	10. transferable

Part 2. Multiple Choice

1. B   2. B   3. E   4. E   5. C   6. D   7. C   8. B   9. D   10. A

Part 3. True or False

1. T   2. F   3. F   4. T   5. F   6. F   7. F   8. F   9. T   10. T

Answers for Chapter 8

Part 1. Fill in the Blank

1. questions
2. appraisal
3. delegates
4. grievance
5. probationary
6. Disciplinary
7. jargon
8. suspended
9. stress
10. personnel

Part 2. Multiple Choice

1. E   2. B   3. C   4. A   5. C   6. D   7. D   8. A   9. E   10. C

Part 3. True or False

1. T   2. F   3. F   4. T   5. F   6. T   7. T   8. F   9. T   10. F

Answers for Chapter 9

Part 1. Fill in the Blank

1. group standards
2. electronic
3. firing
4. team
5. stronger
6. Synergy
7. privacy
8. values
9. diversity
10. sexual

Part 2. Multiple Choice

1. D   2. B   3. D   4. C   5. D   6. A   7. B   8. C   9. E   10. A

Part 3. True or False

1. F   2. T   3. T   4. F   5. T   6. T   7. F   8. T   9. F   10. F

Answers for Chapter 10

Part 1. Fill in the Blank

1. skill
2. lose
3. serving
4. listening
5. greeting
6. attitude
7. hug
8. customer service
9. complaint
10. supervisor

Part 2. Multiple Choice

1. D   2. C   3. D   4. E   5. B   6. D   7. E   8. A   9. E   10. E

Part 3. True or False

1. F   2. T   3. T   4. F   5. T   6. T   7. F   8. F   9. T   10. T

Answers for Chapter 11

Part 1. Fill in the Blank

1. managers
2. identify
3. creative
4. rating/ranking
5. trade journals
6. analysis
7. problem-solving
8. motivated
9. involvement
10. quality

Part 2. Multiple Choice

1. C   2. D   3. B   4. D   5. B   6. A   7. C   8. E   9. E   10. C

Part 3. True or False

1. F   2. T   3. F   4. T   5. T   6. T   7. F   8. F   9. T   10. T

Answers for Chapter 12

Part 1. Fill in the Blank

1. Unethical
2. laws
3. piracy
4. ethics
5. confidential information
6. policy manual
7. illegally
8. self-esteem
9. termination
10. adults

Part 2. Multiple Choice

1. D   2. C   3. B   4. A   5. D   6. E   7. A   8. D   9. E   10. B

Part 3. True or False

1. T   2. F   3. T   4. F   5. F   6. F   7. T   8. T   9. T   10. F

Answers for Chapter 13

Part 1. Fill in the Blank

1. seniority
2. merit
3. promoted
4. career
5. salary
6. wage
7. mentor
8. resignation
9. cost-of-living
10. posting

Part 2. Multiple Choice

1. D   2. E   3. C   4. D   5. B   6. C   7. C   8. E   9. E   10. B

Part 3. True or False

1. T   2. F   3. F   4. T   5. T   6. T   7. F   8. F   9. F   10. T

High School Career Exploration Package (LP-3C9)

Interest Level
5 6 **7 8 9 10 11 12 Adult**

Perfect for initial career exploration and high-school planning for younger high-school students. Package includes Pathfinder *workbooks,* Teacher's Guide, Individual Career Portfolio, *and* JIST's Multimedia OOH CD-ROM *software.*

> *NOTE: ALL* Pathfinder *components and activities*
> * *Meet National Career Development Guidelines*
> * *Reading level of grade 8*

Pathfinder Career Interest Assessment
(30-minute test time)
* Included in workbook—separate purchase unnecessary
* Cross-references **GOE** interest area codes, ties directly to many career reference materials

Pathfinder workbook, 2nd Edition (120 pages)
* Sources of career and educational planning information
* Educational paths
* Pre-employment tests
* Core academic abilities
* Exploring tech prep and college paths

Pathfinder Teacher's Guide, 2nd Edition (64 pages)
* Lesson plans for all **Pathfinder** activities
* Includes supplemental activities, outside assignments, goals for each session, tips for infusing in other classes
* Step-by-step format reduces preparation time

Individual Career Portfolio (6-panel, file folder format)
* Summarizes employability skills
* Documents test results, career choices, academic achievements, awards, extracurricular activities
* Specific high school course planning

JIST's Multimedia OOH CD-ROM
* Complete narratives and photos from the current **Occupational Outlook Handbook (OOH)**
* Thirty (30) video clips (totaling nearly 45 minutes) represent the 9 clusters of **OOH** jobs
* Search by education, salary, outlook, and custom criteria
* More than 20 lists of America's top jobs for college grads, including graduates of community colleges, trade schools, etc.

HIGH SCHOOL CAREER EXPLORATION PACKAGE (LP-3C9)

25 .... Pathfinder workbooks, 2nd Edition (LP-J5249)

1 .... Pathfinder Teacher's Guide, 2nd Edition (LP-J5257)

1 pkg* ...... Individual Career Portfolios (LP-JA546X)

1 .... JIST's Multimedia OOH CD-ROM (LP-JS5389)

High School Career Exploration Package (LP-3C9) Price: $482.65

* One package = 25 copies

High School Job Search Package (LP-4C9)

An excellent package for students learning how to find jobs.
Includes Getting the Job You Really Want *workbook and*
Instructor's Guide, *the* Job Search Attitude Inventory, *and the*
Video Guide to Summer and Part-Time Jobs.

Interest Level
5 6 7 8 9 10 11 12 Adult

The Job Search Attitude Inventory—JSAI (30-minute test time)
- Identifies positive and negative job search attitudes
- Identifies the degree to which students believe they have control over finding jobs
- Use as pre- and post-test

Guide for Occupational Exploration (GOE) Inventory
(30-minute test time)
A quick, intuitive assessment that relates work values, home activities, work settings, leisure/volunteer activities, and education/training to the 12 GOE occupational clusters.
- Excellent for students and people with little or no work experience
- Group administered, self-scored, immediate results
- Direct cross-references to a wealth of information

Getting the Job You Really Want, 3rd Edition (202 pages)
An excellent workbook that's sold more than 220,000 copies!
- The very best self-directed job search techniques
- Students learn how to organize and take charge
- Good graphics
- Lots of in-the-book activities, charts, skills checklists
- Details on more than 200 major jobs!
- Structures a course when used with instructor's guide
- Reading level: grades 8–9

Getting the Job You Really Want Instructor's Guide (64 pages)
- Lesson plans for multiple sessions
- Individual and group activities
- Supplemental handouts
- Homework assignments
- Discussion and quiz questions

Video Guide to Summer and Part-Time Jobs (20 minutes)
- Young people discuss their work experiences, both good and bad
- Explores reasons—aside from money—for seeking summer and part-time jobs
- Cautions about potential negative impact on school performance
- Discusses career benefits of jobs, internships, and volunteer work

The Pocket Book of Job Search Data & Tips (32 pages)
Good things DO come in small packages! Now there's a condensed, convenient, complete record-storing reference system to organize personal job histories. At 3.5" x 5", it fits in virtually any pocket or handbag. Job seekers always have key data and information about themselves at their fingertips for completing job applications, preparing for interviews, and writing resumes.

HIGH SCHOOL JOB SEARCH PACKAGE
(LP-4C9)

25 .... Getting the Job You Really Want
                 workbooks (LP-RWR)

1 .... Getting the Job You Really Want
                 Instructor's Guide (LP-RWRIG)

1 .... JIST Career Planning/Job Search Course
                 Transparency Set—
                 52 transparencies (JSCT)

1 pkg* ...... Job Search Attitude Inventory (LP-JSAI)

1 .... Video Guide to Summer and
                 Part-Time Jobs (LP-JV4870)

1 pkg* ...... Guide for Occupational Exploration
                 Inventory (LP-JA2452)

25 .... The Pocket Book of Job Search Data &
                 Tips (LP-J3092)

High School Job Search Package
(LP-4C9) Price: $522.35

* One package = 25 copies

School-to-Work On-Site Training Workshop** (LP-16C9)
Employability Planning and Job Search Methods for High School Students

A one-day, train-the-trainer workshop for educational professionals who help students plan careers.

Interest Level
5 6 7 8 9 10 11 12 Adult

All employers want workers who communicate effectively, interact well with others, and demonstrate positive attitudes toward themselves and their jobs. These employability skills can—and should be—mastered well before students accept their first jobs. In this school-to-career workshop, educators learn how to prepare students for the world of work.

Agenda Highlights
- Learning a skills language
- Identifying skills
- "Why should I hire you?"
- Career exploration/interest inventories
- Taking ownership of your job and your life
- Putting skills to use
- Applications and resumes
- Developing effective interview strategies
- Job retention skills/being successful on the job
- Problem solving/ethics

Who Should Attend?
High school counselors, administrators, teachers, school-to-work coordinators, and other educational professionals who help students plan careers. Ideal for school-to-work programs, at-risk youth programs, summer youth programs, and correctional youth education programs.

For detailed workshop agenda and booking information, contact Janet Banks, Training Director, at 1-800-547-8366.

JIST Training Institute offers several other on-site workshops**

- **Career Planning and Self-Directed Job Search Workshop**
- **Workplace Readiness: Helping People Prepare for Success on the Job**
- **From Dream to Reality: Starting Your Small Business**
- **Using the Internet and the World Wide Web in Your Job Search**

***Workshop held at your location**

SCHOOL-TO-WORK TRAINING WORKSHOP PACKAGE FOR 25 ATTENDEES (LP-16C9)

The price of this one-day workshop includes the following products (valued at $165.00 per person):

25	Young Person's Guide to Getting & Keeping a Good Job workbook (LP-YP)
25	Young Person's Guide to Getting & Keeping a Good Job Instructor's Guide (LP-YPTM)
25	Young Person's Guide to Getting & Keeping a Good Job Overhead Transparencies (LP-YPTRAN)
25	Job Savvy, 2nd Edition workbook (LP-J3041)
25	Job Savvy Instructor's Guide, 2nd Edition (LP-J4358)
25	Job Savvy Overhead Transparencies (LP-J4463)
1 pkg*	Career Exploration Inventory (LP-CEI)
1 pkg*	Leisure/Work Search Inventory (LP-LSI)

School-to-Work Training Workshop (LP-16C9)
Price: $7,500.00 for <u>25 people</u>
Group sizes that are 26 to 40 people will be charged $185.00 per person over the initial 25 attendees.

One package = 25 copies

JIST Order Form

| Please copy this form if you |
| need more lines for your order. |

Purchase Order #: _____ (Required by some organizations)

Billing Information
Organization Name: _____
Accounting Contact: _____
Street Address: _____
_____
_____
City, State, Zip: _____
Phone Number: ( ) _____

Shipping Information with Street Address (If Different from Above)
Organization Name: _____
Contact: _____
Street Address: (We *cannot* ship to P.O. boxes) _____
_____
City, State, Zip: _____
Phone Number: ( ) _____

Credit Card Purchases: VISA____ MC____ AMEX____
Card Number: _____
Exp. Date: _____
Name As on Card: _____
Signature: _____

Quantity	Order Code	Product Title	Unit Price	Total

Subtotal	
+5% Sales Tax *Indiana Residents*	
+Shipping / Handling / Ins. (See left)	
TOTAL	

jist Works, Inc.
8902 Otis Avenue
Indianapolis, IN 46216

Practical, self-directed tools and training for career explorers and job seekers of all ages!

Shipping / Handling / Insurance Fees

In the continental U.S. add 7% of subtotal:
- Minimum amount charged = $4.00
- Maximum amount charged = $100.00
- FREE shipping and handling on any prepaid orders over $40.00.
Above pricing is for regular ground shipment only. For rush or special delivery, call JIST Customer Service at 1-800-648-JIST for the correct shipping fee.

Outside the continental U.S. call JIST Customer Service at 1-800-648-JIST for an estimate of these fees.

Payment in U.S. funds only!

JIST thanks you for your order!